"*The Way of the Kingdom* is a b
heart of Christianity and provi(
need in troubled times. It is full of wisdom to bring life-saving
knowledge as well as points of reflection. Kim Maas can write
on such subjects as suffering, peace and redemption because
she has lived that message personally. Prepare to be changed,
challenged and inspired!"

Cindy Jacobs, founder, Generals International

"Kim Maas presents a brilliant profile of the times we are living in and how to position ourselves in such an hour. You will
discover many revelatory keys in her book, *The Way of the Kingdom*, that will open the eyes of your understanding to God's
purpose, plan and power for this generation of believers."

Dr. Patricia King, author, minister, television host

"There is an unseen enemy and demonic campaign against
God's plan and His people. Kim Maas's powerful book, *The
Way of the Kingdom*, decodes the mysteries of Christ's Kingdom
by unleashing prophetic revelatory insight, imparting biblical truths and activating the rules-of-engagement strategies
against the kingdom of darkness for victorious living for every
believer."

Dr. Hakeem Collins, prophetic voice;
international speaker; author, *10 Prayer Secrets*

"*The Way of the Kingdom* offers breakthrough insights into the
very essence of Christianity—a Christianity from Jesus, the
founder, and what He emphasized. This work is not simply a
new theology. It joyously commends the mission and message
of Jesus Himself to any who would follow Him."

Dr. Jon Mark Ruthven, Ph.D. curriculum creator,
Iris University, Pemba, Mozambique

"I have never met Kim Maas, but when I read her book *The
Way of the Kingdom*, I knew her heart. Few times have I picked
up a book that conveyed a better understanding of the Lord's

statement that the least in the Kingdom would be greater than John the Baptist. What you hold in your hands will help you make the divine shift and transfer your mind-set to move outwardly into God's Kingdom plan to align heaven with earth today."

Dr. Chuck D. Pierce, president, Glory of Zion International
Ministries; president, Global Spheres

"In this inspiring and enlightening book, Kim Maas reminds us that we have entered a new season, and how we respond during this time matters deeply to God. Each chapter contains practical activations and thoughtful questions that will help you discover your role and responsibility during this epoch time in history. I recommend this book to anyone seeking strategies to demolish darkness and advance God's Kingdom!"

Kris Vallotton, senior associate leader, Bethel Church;
co-founder, Bethel School of Supernatural Ministry;
bestselling author, *Spiritual Intelligence*

"Jesus commands us all to 'go!' With revelations from Scripture, soul-searching questions and activations, *The Way of the Kingdom* challenges us to go—to the grocery store, the library, the workplace and even to Africa. This book will help you respond to Jesus with an enthusiastic yes!"

Heidi G. Baker, Ph.D., co-founder and executive
chairman of the board, Iris Global

"To overcome the darkness from generation to generation, we must understand not only the operations of darkness but also the operations of the Kingdom of God. This book will help you to sharpen your war weapons and rise to new levels of victory through faith."

Dr. Venner J. Alston, founder, Alston International Ministries;
author, *Next-Level Spiritual Warfare*

THE WAY OF THE
KINGDOM

Seizing the Times for a GREAT MOVE of God

KIM M. MAAS

Chosen

a division of Baker Publishing Group
Minneapolis, Minnesota

Published by Chosen Books
11400 Hampshire Avenue South
Bloomington, Minnesota 55438
www.chosenbooks.com

Chosen Books is a division of
Baker Publishing Group, Grand Rapids, Michigan

Printed in the United States of America

Library of Congress Cataloging-in-Publication Data
Names: Maas, Kim M., author.
Title: The way of the kingdom : seizing the times for a great move of God / Kim
    Marie Maas.
Description: Minneapolis, Minnesota : Chosen Books, a division of Baker
    Publishing Group, 2021. | Includes bibliographical references.
Identifiers: LCCN 2021006114 | ISBN 9780800799328 (trade paper) | ISBN
    9780800762339 (casebound) | ISBN 9781493431281 (ebook)
Subjects: LCSH: Kingdom of God. | Spiritual warfare. | Violence—Religious
    aspects—Christianity. | Church and the world. | Christianity and culture.
Classification: LCC BT94 .M223 2021 | DDC 231.7/2—dc23
LC record available at https://lccn.loc.gov/2021006114

Cover design by LOOK Design Studio

21 22 23 24 25 26 27   7 6 5 4 3 2 1

For Ian, Jameson, Camron, Macallan and Seth.

Follow Jesus. Be Brave.
Do damage to the kingdom of darkness.
Remember that you are salt and light,
and you are bringers of the powerful Kingdom of God.
Grandma loves you so, so much.

Contents

Foreword

God, after He spoke long ago to the fathers in the prophets
in many portions and in many ways, in these last days has
spoken to us in His Son, whom He appointed heir of all things,
through whom He also made the world.

Hebrews 1:1–2 NASB

The writer of Hebrews informs us that God has spoken in His Son. You and I perhaps are bilingual. We may speak English and another language. God only speaks one language. He speaks "Son." It is the very testimony of Jesus that is the spirit of prophecy. Jesus is the main event. The fullness of times is experienced in Him, in His very being. He is God's eternal and ultimate Word.

As C. E. W. Green has said, "Nothing happens to God. God happens to everything." When the incarnation occurred, time itself underwent change. Mary's boy, conceived of the Holy Spirit in her womb, was the divine Person assuming human flesh. Saint Athanasius, in *On the Incarnation of the Word*, makes it clear: "He became what we are that we might become what he is."

This is not an easy pill to swallow for us in our broken and fragmented state. We resist the cross-shaped life, the very life that Christ brings. Yet this is the testimony of Jesus. If it isn't cross-shaped (if it isn't cruciform), it isn't the spirit of prophecy. The Spirit only testifies of Christ in His cross-shaped realities. Jesus calls us all to follow Him, in like manner, on the journey to becoming fully and truly human.

The cross and the cross-shaped life are a scandalous thing. It is reverse violence. It is the difficult journey of birthing something new through the pain of travail. Pain and suffering are two of the many companions that lead us into deeper intimacy and communion with God in His triune life.

It is at the cross where Jesus perfectly reveals who the Father is in His love toward us. Hence, the Kingdom suffers violence, and the violent embrace that cross, and through the birth pangs of sorrow and travail, the expression of the government of God is brought into every sphere of life.

This story is well rehearsed and well told over the course of two millennia. The key is for you and I to live in this story and see ourselves precisely as those who are easily scandalized by the cross-shaped life. How then do we now live?

The book you hold in your hand is one pathway there. Kim Maas has taken time to talk to us about the way of the Kingdom. While the pathway involves signs and wonders that confirm its declaration, it does not come without pain and suffering. That is something that is not popular in a postmodern era where the truth is up for grabs and there are seemingly no absolutes. In these pages, Kim offers to accompany you on a journey that grounds us each step of the way in how to take the next, easiest step in following Jesus through our brokenness to His wholeness, from our fragmentation to a place of integrity.

Her writing is clear and easily accessible. When I was learning how to preach, practicing on various congregations, the mothers of the churches would shout back at me, "Make it plain." Kim makes it plain.

Kim is going to take you into the very heart of your existence in Christ, and the cross-shaped journey that is all too easy to avoid in a day when selfish pleasure, ambition, and what's-in-it-for-me have clouded our vision and hindered our testimony. Take your time, listen deeply, and have ears to hear.

Thanks, Kim, for your voice!

Bishop Mark J. Chironna, senior pastor, Church on the Living Edge; founder, Mark Chironna Ministries

Acknowledgments

My Jesus, the One who overcomes darkness violently, thank You. My husband, Michael Maas, the one who overcomes the dishes and dullness of everyday life, thank you. My acquisition editor, Kim Bangs, the one who overcomes the terror and intimidation I experience in writing, thank you. I could not have done this without any of you.

Prologue

The first six chapters of this book include a prophetic interpretation and biblical exegesis of a passage of Scripture taken from the Holy Bible found in Matthew 11, with a focus on verse 12. I have written out the passage in its entirety—verses 1 to 15—for ease of reference.

When Jesus had finished instructing his twelve disciples, he went on from there to teach and preach in their cities.

Now when John heard in prison about the deeds of the Christ, he sent word by his disciples and said to him, "Are you the one who is to come, or shall we look for another?" And Jesus answered them, "Go and tell John what you hear and see: the blind receive their sight and the lame walk, lepers are cleansed and the deaf hear, and the dead are raised up, and the poor have good news preached to them. And blessed is the one who is not offended by me."

As they went away, Jesus began to speak to the crowds concerning John: "What did you go out into the wilderness to see? A reed shaken by the wind? What then did you go out to see? A man dressed in soft clothing? Behold, those who wear soft clothing are in kings' houses. What then did you go out to see? A prophet? Yes, I tell you, and more than a prophet. This is he of whom it is written, 'Behold, I send my messenger before your face, who will prepare your way before you.' Truly, I say to you, among those born of women there has arisen no one greater than John the Baptist. Yet the one who is least in the kingdom of heaven is greater than he. From the days of John the Baptist until now the kingdom of heaven has suffered violence, and the violent take it by force. For all the Prophets and the Law prophesied until John, and if you are willing to accept it, he is Elijah who is to come. He who has ears to hear, let him hear.

"But to what shall I compare this generation? It is like children sitting in the marketplaces and calling to their playmates, 'We played the flute for you, and you did not dance; we sang a dirge, and you did not mourn.' For John came neither eating nor drinking, and they say, 'He has a demon.' The Son of Man came eating and drinking, and they say, 'Look at him! A glutton and a drunkard, a friend of tax collectors and sinners!' Yet wisdom is justified by her deeds."

Let's pray. Father, Your Word never returns void, it never falls short of Your intentions, it never misses its mark and it never fades in potency or immediacy. Holy Spirit, come breathe afresh on Your Word and on all who read it. May it penetrate heart, soul, mind and body and produce its rich reward—truth that sets people free. Give us ears to hear what the Spirit is saying so that we do not miss the time of our visitation. Give us Your eternal Word for our present need and for eternity. In Jesus' name, Amen.

Introduction

Of Issachar, *men who had understanding of the times, to know what Israel ought to do*, 200 chiefs, and all their kinsmen under their command.

1 Chronicles 12:32, emphasis added

Therefore *do not throw away your confidence*, which has a great reward. For *you have need of endurance*, so that when you have done the will of God you may receive what is promised.

Hebrews 10:35–36, emphasis added

In February 2017, I had a prophetic dream. In this dream, I was attending a World Heavyweight Championship boxing match. The two fighters were standing near me about to get into the ring. One walked right past me. The other was a man I recognized. He had been a well-known prizefighter who could not presently be in his prime. In my dream, however, he was strong, fit and muscular. I asked him how he had made his comeback.

He said, "Through diligence, training and a very strict routine." His body looked young and virile. You could see age in his face, but he was not tired.

As the fight started, my perspective became as if I were part of the media and I was watching the fight through a camera. The camera I was viewing through panned across the ring and the crowd. As it passed over the crowd, I caught a glimpse of a woman who was standing ringside dressed as a geisha. She was holding a gun straight out in front of her. The camera had passed by her, and then went back suddenly and focused on her.

I heard a voice say, "A gun! She has a gun!" Just then, the gun went off, and I saw the bullet come from the gun in slow motion. I knew it had missed its target—and then the dream ended.

As I was waking from the dream, the Lord said, *Jezebel has waged war against the Church.* He went on to explain to me that the two fighters represented the cultural struggle and violent division the Church is experiencing as a result of a compromised Gospel.

I have often heard the term *religious* thrown out with a scoff as it is used to label any practice of spiritual discipline as ridiculous and outdated. There are worship leaders, for example, who get drunk on alcohol backstage before a worship concert. There are pastors who use foul language. There are leaders in government and in the Church who dabble with drug use and participate in entertainment that degrades women, promotes promiscuity, mocks adultery and encourages every kind of sexual perversion and violence.

No matter how wealthy, educated, thin, powerful or sexually liberated we have become, we are poverty stricken in our souls. We are sin-sick in our personal lives, our families and the world. We are desperately alone and unhappy. And yet we are being called into a fight, and it is surely the heavyweight championship of the world. It is a battle for our nation, for the Church and for the next generation.

All is not lost! God is awakening His Church. She is represented by the prizefighter of old—the awakened Body of Christ. God is making her fit, formidable and muscle-bound. She is about to step into the ring and make a comeback to win this war.

It is time that we see the big picture. If we do not, we will get caught up in distractions, miss the greater purpose and have a difficult time moving forward. When times get tough—and they always do—the temptation to quit will overcome us. It is not, however, time to quit. It is time to stand and advance the Kingdom of God.

Something in the air is new. An extraordinary thing is about to happen, and we are living in the moment just before it comes. We have not been this way before. Jesus, however, is waiting in the extraordinary thing. He will be with us in the future as He is with us now. Always.

This is a very serious and sobering time. This new movement will have extraordinary consequences. It will include cleansing, purification and holiness that will expose compromise and sin, as well as release great power and authority. It will prove to be a time when the people of God will once again know the fear of the Lord. We cannot serve the culture and political correctness and still take our place in the Kingdom. It is time to think and act as Kingdom people.

When governments shift and nations are shaken, everything changes and history is made. It is God at work. It is God who changes times and seasons, who removes and sets up kings, and who gives wisdom and understanding about deep and hidden things we could not otherwise know (see Daniel 2:21–22). It is God who is working actively in every circumstance to bring about His will on earth as it is in heaven (see Matthew 6:10).

The shifts, sudden changes and even crises will create unprecedented opportunities for Kingdom advancement if we become shrewd in personal finance, business, politics and, yes, even ministry. Remember, if nothing changes, then nothing changes. These situations will be the impetus for change so that we can seize the opportunities and advance the Kingdom.

The Time Is Now

History, including each and every era, is ordered divinely. There is a time for all things, and each thing is decided by God. What is more, for every divinely ordered season there is an appropriate corresponding action. This is what the preacher in Ecclesiastes wants us to understand.

> For everything there is a season, and a time for every matter under heaven:
>
>> a time to be born, and a time to die; a time to plant, and a time to pluck up what is planted; a time to kill, and a time to heal; a time to break down, and a time to build up; a time to weep, and a time to laugh; a time to mourn, and a time to dance; a time to cast away stones, and a time to gather stones together; a time to embrace, and a time to refrain from embracing; a time to seek, and a time to lose; a time to keep, and a time to cast away; a time to tear, and a time to sew; a time to keep silence, and a time to speak; a time to love, and a time to hate; a time for war, and a time for peace.
>
> Ecclesiastes 3:1–8

In Luke, Jesus calls those who identify themselves as God's people hypocrites. He explains that they are able to interpret seasonal weather patterns but are not able to interpret the times and seasons of God (see Luke 12:54–56). In Matthew, He chastises the Pharisees and Sadducees for not being able to interpret the signs of the times (see Matthew 16:2–3). Since they are unable to read the signs of the times, they miss the divinely appointed season; therefore, they do not take the appropriate action or lead others to do so. They are blind guides.

There are many seasons referenced in Scripture, and each one overlaps and is interwoven in God's plan and agenda. They are not linear or compartmentalized. It is God's desire that we are aware of these times and seasons so that we may engage in the divinely appointed activities appropriate to them.

One of those is *chronos time*, which is expressed by our calendars and is marked by the movement of the planets, stars, sun and moon. Days, years, and seedtimes and harvests are examples of *chronos* time. This time is the chronological history in which we find the acts of God among men. What is the right action for God's people in *chronos* time? We are to understand and learn God's ways.

There is also *Kingdom time*, which encompasses what the Bible calls the last days or the *eschatos*. The last days began with the coming of Jesus in the flesh (see Hebrews 1:2), are marked by the outpouring of the Holy Spirit (see Acts 2:17), and await the coming of Christ once more when all of His enemies are conquered and the final trumpet sounds (see 1 Corinthians 15:26–27, 52).

The *Dictionary of Biblical Imagery* calls this time *eschatological time*, or the time of salvation, where the focus is not on the past or the future but on the present.[1] "Behold, now is the favorable time; behold, now is the day of salvation" (2 Corinthians 6:2). In Kingdom time, we are living in the season when salvation has come to humankind through the life, death and resurrection of Christ and through the outpouring and supernatural empowerment of the Holy Spirit. The right action for this time is to be born again, to be filled with the Spirit and to be about the business of completing His mission on earth.

According to the prophet Isaiah, there is also a *now time*. "Behold, I am doing a new thing; *now* it springs forth, do you not perceive it?" (Isaiah 43:19, emphasis added). Now time is a season of intervention when God introduces change. Not every new thing is God's intervention. We need to look to God and watch for His work. This requires that we know His Word, His ways and His voice. The right action in a now time is to let go of the past and embrace the new thing God is bringing.

Another time is *prophetic time*, which we find in the foretelling of the prophetic books in Scripture. Foretelling in prophecy is foreseeing the future. God speaks to His people about what will be, giving them direction on how to navigate that season. This means that the future has implications for the present. Acting on those implications to prepare for the future that God has designed is the right action to take.

There is also *kairos time*. This is a term we often hear used in the charismatic community. Although its meaning is varied, it is used commonly to indicate a time of crisis and divine opportunity. It is a season when God opens an opportune door (or some would say a window), usually through a crisis or sudden change. A *kairos* time has a specific beginning and ending. In other words, the opportunity that comes in a *kairos* time can be missed. This is a time to make a decision and act. *Carpe diem*.

Times and seasons are the testing ground for people's spiritual identities. If we are truly the people of God, then we have been given the ability (by the Spirit) to know and interpret the time and season we are in. This revelatory knowledge is given to inform our decisions so that we may take the right action in every divinely appointed season. Moreover, we will have answers and solutions for the times in order to help others.

In Jeremiah, the Lord utters a painful rebuke to Israel, who, unlike the stork, did not know their appointed time with its appropriate action:

"Even the stork in the heavens knows her times, and the turtle-dove, swallow, and crane keep the time of their coming, but my people know not the rules of the LORD. . . . They have healed the wound of my people lightly, saying, 'Peace, peace,' when there is no peace."

Jeremiah 8:7, 11

There is a right action for every divinely appointed season. Will we be as the stork? Or will we, the Body of Christ, be as those who take lightly the hardship of the times and offer wrong answers and solutions to those who are wounded? Let it never be said of us! Our identity as the Body of Christ means that we are the ones who have the ability to understand the times and seasons, and we are the ones who can know the right action to take. In other words, we are the New Testament version of the men of Issachar (see 1 Chronicles 12:32).

What are the signs of our time? Look around. There is shaking, volatility and violence in the world in the form of child abuse, terrorism, economic crisis, geopolitical power struggles, racism, persecution, pandemics, divorce, abortion and cancer. We are living in violent times. The world is changing, nations are vying for power and culture is becoming more and more suspicious of those who profess faith in Christ. It should be no surprise. The unrest and opposition we are experiencing in the world are a sign of the Spirit of God on the move. How do we know? How do we respond?

The answer is found in Jesus' ominous words: "From the days of John the Baptist until now the kingdom of heaven has suffered violence, and the violent take it by force" (Matthew 11:12). Why did He say it? What does it mean? What do we do?

In *The Way of the Kingdom*, we will explore these questions and more. Going through this book will prepare us, as the Body of Christ, to be a force to be reckoned with. We will learn to become the violent ones who do acts of Kingdom violence.

Answering violence with violence sounds like war. It is. We are in a war. Yet the violence of the world is nothing like Kingdom violence. This book will explain the difference.

In chapter 1, we will investigate what caused John the Baptist, the fiery prophet, to ask Jesus a strange question in Matthew 11. In chapters 2–5, we will learn about the way of the Kingdom. Jesus is leading a violent breakout from the prison that is fashioned in darkness. The prince of darkness is leading a violent breakout in opposition to it. Distinguishing the violence of the world from the violence of the Kingdom empowers us to advance effectively the Kingdom of God as the Body of Christ. We will explore this in chapter 6.

In chapters 7–9, we will hear Jesus offer us His peace and remind us that death has lost its sting. This knowledge should unlock fearlessness in us so that we can face violent times. Finally, in chapter 10, we will be challenged by Jesus as we are commissioned into the world to be a part of the spiritual revolution God intends for our time. It is time for us to understand the way of the Kingdom as those who seize the times for a great move of God!

The violent times are a sign to us. Not the kind of sign you may think. Violence is a response to the movement of the Spirit. When the Kingdom of God encroaches into the territories ruled by darkness, violence is the manifestation of the warfare. God, His Kingdom and His people are advancing. Violent times are a sign of a coming fresh awakening. We are about to see a demonstration of the Gospel in this next generation as no generation before us has ever seen. Revival has begun! God is moving, and we are being called to awaken to our task without fear.

CHAPTER 1

Are You the One?

"Are you the one who is to come, or shall we look for another?"

Matthew 11:3

"We are closer to God when we are asking questions than when we think we have the answers."

Abraham Joshua Heschel

The senior pastor asked the congregation to pray for those whose hands were raised to acknowledge that they needed healing. As I turned around, I noticed a tattooed man with colorful hair who was in the far back of the room. I walked over to him and asked if I could pray for him. He seemed uncomfortable, but he complied.

He had raised his hand to receive healing for back pain. As I laid my hands on him, I felt depressed. I knew that the emotion I was feeling was his emotion and not mine. I began to ask the Lord what the depression was related to, and I received a word of knowledge. A word of knowledge is a supernatural revelation of information that comes from the Holy Spirit apart from natural analysis or human means. I find that the Holy Spirit will often give me a word of knowledge for a specific need in relation to healing—whether physical, emotional or relational—to provide more specified and targeted ministry. In this man's case, I heard in my mind and heart that the man had experienced a relationship breakup that had not been resolved.

I said, "The Lord is showing me that you have been suffering with depression." He burst into tears, and I prayed for healing in his body, in his heart and in his relationship.

Weeks later, I returned to that church. When worship ended, a testimony video started. A man who was cleanly shaven graced the screen to tell a miraculous story. Several weeks prior, he had visited the church for the first time after being invited repeatedly by his friend. He came reluctantly and sat in the back. That morning the pastor asked if anyone needed healing for anything in his or her body. The man in the video said that he had needed many things in his body healed, but he had not wanted to raise his hand. The friend who had invited him encouraged him to do it, and he did hesitantly.

The man said, "A woman named Kim turned and saw me and made her way to me." It was then that I realized this was the tattooed man that I had prayed for. He looked completely different.

He told how he had lost his wife, his health, his job, his dignity and his will to live. He not only had back pain that forced him to walk with a walker or a cane, but he also had cancer. On any given day, it would take him hours to get out of bed and care for himself. He was depressed, bitter and angry.

The morning after he had come to church and received prayer, he stepped out of his bed and felt no pain. He got dressed and ran around the block. Still, no pain. The following day, he received a job offer with good pay. Within a few weeks, he was cleared by his doctor of all health issues and had given his heart to Jesus. He had a whole new life. The changes were so profound and miraculous that he made a decision to become a chaplain to bring the power of God to others. He knew the enemy had tried to take him out for good. Jesus had another plan.

Violence Is Nothing New

Intimidation and violence have always been the name of the enemy's game. Scripture tells us that Satan comes to kill, steal and destroy (see John 10:10). As real as the Kingdom of heaven is, there is also a real counterfeit kingdom. It is a kingdom of darkness that is moving on the earth attempting to strike fear in the hearts of all who refuse to bow down to the gods of this age.

Violence and violent times are not a surprise to God. He is not seated on His throne wringing His hands in anxiety wondering what to do. God uses circumstances and events to stretch, challenge, test, squeeze and pressurize us. He turns up the heat around us so that what is in us—our faith and character—comes to the surface. We hear Peter explain that fiery trials are a means of proving our faith. This process results in praise and glory for Jesus (see 1 Peter 4:13). James says we are to be grateful for the trials that test our faith because they produce endurance (see James 1:2–4). So then, we know our faith is being tested by these challenges, and these challenges are producing endurance that God will use to help us receive His fulfilled promises.

From the beginning of its inauguration, the Kingdom of God has suffered violence. Jesus said so: "From the days of John the Baptist until now the kingdom of heaven suffers violence, and the violent take it by force" (Matthew 11:12 NKJV). Matthew records what Jesus said to those who were facing violence.

"And you will hear of wars and rumors of wars. See that you are not alarmed, for this must take place, but the end is not yet. For nation will rise against nation, and kingdom against kingdom, and there will be famines and earthquakes in various places."

Matthew 24:6–7

Did John Not Know Jesus Was the One?

When we read that John questions Jesus' identity it is stunning. John was Jesus' cousin, which means they knew of the miracles surrounding each other's birth. In a religious tradition that kept scrupulous accounts of family history by verbal transmission, they must have known the stories. Now, launched fully into their ministries, both John and Jesus have been announcing confidently that the Kingdom is at hand. They seem to be on the same page.

Unexpectedly, however, John sent his disciples to ask Jesus, "Are you the one who is to come, or shall we look for another?" (Matthew 11:3). Wait, what? Did John not know? We thought he knew. It sure seemed as though he knew. Now he seems confused.

Is this not John, as in John *the Baptist*? Is this not John, the John who is "the voice of one crying in the wilderness" sent to prepare the way of the Lord?[1] In fact, in the gospel of John (the Beloved, not the Baptist) we read that when asked if he was Elijah returned from the dead, John the Baptist identified himself as the voice crying out in the wilderness. He knew he was the fulfillment of Isaiah's prophesy.

Is John not a prophet? The prophet was the voice of God. He was a mouthpiece and a spokesman who declared God's message about the present and the future to the people, their leaders and the nations in a terrifying and absurd world. According to Jewish scholar Abraham Heschel, "The prophet was an individual who said *no* to his society, condemning its habits and assumptions, its

28

complacency, waywardness, and syncretism. . . . His fundamental objective was to reconcile man to God."[2] John, as a prophet who had been called to prepare the way of the Lord, urged Israel to repent and return to covenant relationship with God through baptism before the fires of judgment overtook them. He knew he was a prophet. He knew he was not the Christ (see John 1:20).

Is John not the one who announced Jesus as the coming Messiah? Did he not receive from God a sign he could use to identify the Son of God, the Savior and the baptizer with the Holy Spirit?

> The next day he saw Jesus coming toward him, and said, "Behold, the Lamb of God, who takes away the sin of the world! This is he of whom I said, 'After me comes a man who ranks before me, because he was before me.' I myself did not know him, but for this purpose I came baptizing with water, that he might be revealed to Israel." And John bore witness: "I saw the Spirit descend from heaven like a dove, and it remained on him. I myself did not know him, but he who sent me to baptize with water said to me, 'He on whom you see the Spirit descend and remain, this is he who baptizes with the Holy Spirit.' *And I have seen and have borne witness that this is the Son of God.*"
>
> John 1:29–36, emphasis added

Yes, he is that John—John the Baptizer who baptized Jesus in the Jordan. He is the one who witnessed the sign from heaven, which was the Spirit descending upon Jesus and the word that confirmed Jesus' identity. John knew he was the witness giving the testimony of Jesus as the One. Even when His disciples questioned him about his ministry diminishing, John reiterated, "I am not the Christ. . . . He must increase, but I must decrease" (John 3:28, 30).

Both Jesus and John were on the forefront leading a revival and a fresh move of God. John was calling Israel to get ready for a new season in which God was stepping in to establish His Kingdom and His rule. John knew that his assignment was to announce what God was doing and that Jesus was the One God had sent to do it. The Kingdom was coming!

John knew. He thought he knew. Up until this point in the story, we thought he knew, too. Then, without warning, we read how he questioned what he once knew.

"Are you the One who is to come, or shall we look for another?"

Why is John asking if Jesus is the One when John himself declared Jesus to be the One? In order to understand John's question, we need to understand John's expectations.

Expectations are formed (or informed) by our belief systems. Belief systems are created around principles and truths we have trusted; therefore, a set of facts can create expectation. If I am hired to work an eight-hour day at an hourly wage, for example, I expect to be paid for eight hours of work.

Previous experiences can create expectations. If I have tried and failed at every diet known to man, then I will expect to fail at the next latest craze. What we perceive to be plausible in light of what we have believed, assumed, presumed, reasoned or been taught to be true is usually what we will expect to happen.

Expectations come in many shapes and sizes. We all have them. Israel had them. John, as a part of Israel, shared them.

John Expected a New King

As John begins his ministry, we hear him announcing the coming of the Kingdom of heaven. John is announcing that the dominion, sovereignty and rule of God as King on earth as it is in heaven is upon them. The Messianic age is breaking in. Righteousness (right relationship with God) must be reestablished among Israel, who had been exiled by their own sin and covenant breaking. There was an urgency to bring God's people to repentance. They would need to bear the fruit of repentance in concrete behavioral ways if they expected to see the end of exile.

Attending services at the temple was not enough. Circumcision was not enough. It is not enough to clean the outside of a cup. This repentance was about the heart and the life lived out of the heart. John called God's people to repentance. They were to turn from every wicked way that defiled their hearts and lives. They were to be cleansed from sin and get right with God. John was trying to communicate that revival was coming and holiness was required. The King and His Kingdom were at hand!

What John expressed was his expectation of severe and punitive judgment—the wrath of God—coming suddenly on those who were unrepentant and unwilling to change their ways.

John indicts the religious leadership of Israel with a scathing accusation and dire warning of the wrath of God for their hypocrisy (see Matthew 3:1–12). The religious leaders scoff and reject John's offer of baptism for remission of sin. They think they are ready for the coming of the Messiah because they follow strict ritual purity, yet they do not practice mercy or compassion. Remember what Jesus said to the Pharisees: "Go and learn what this means: 'I desire mercy, and not sacrifice'" (Matthew 9:13).

Worse yet was the cruel and corrupt Herod Antipas, the "King of the Jews," who was the ruling monarch in John's territory of Galilee and Parea.[3] He was the son of a murderous king who slaughtered the toddlers of Israel to prevent a divine coup by Jesus.[4]

The kings of Israel were meant to be spiritual leaders. Yet Herod had unlawfully married his brother's wife, who was also his niece, committing a type of incest (see Mark 6:17–18; Matthew 14:3–4). What kind of spirituality was he modeling?

31

In true Old Testament prophetic tradition, John confronts Herod's sin and calls him to repent. He refused. He was a corrupt king.

Interestingly, there was another "king" present in the time of John. Caesar, in Rome, was considered divine. He was called the Son of God. He was considered to be the divine king of Rome (and the whole world, for that matter, as Rome was considered the ruler of the known world). Under Roman rule, Israel suffered severe sociopolitical oppression.

Together, the two so-called kings, Herod and Caesar, embodied the corrupt political and religious systems that were oppressing God's people. John took a stand against them, confronting their corruption and iniquity. Therefore, when John announces the inbreaking of a new Kingdom with a new King sent by God, he was announcing a revolution with religious and sociopolitical consequences. It was disruptive and shocking.

Was he right? Yes and no. The announcement was the word of the Lord. The expectation was skewed. Often a prophetic word comes to pass in a way even the prophet does not expect. John had expectations that were rooted deeply and are worth examining. His expectations were pervasive, and they threatened to blind the whole nation from being able to see the manifestation of their long-awaited hope.

John Expected a Sovereign, Powerful King

In a night vision, the great prophet Daniel saw "one like a son of man" (Daniel 7:13). This Son of man would have a Kingdom, and He would be given dominion, authority and power over all peoples, nations, tribes and tongues. His Kingdom would be indestructible. Revival history buff and founder of the apostolic network Global Awakening, Randy Clark, explains, "This was the popular prophetic understanding of the messiah in the first century for the Jewish people."[5]

Additionally, through the prophet Nathan, God promises to establish the kingdom of David's offspring forever. He promises that He will personally be a father to him (see 2 Samuel 7:12–14). This is a promise of dynasty—a permanent, eternal kingdom. This beautiful and uniquely divine father-son relationship is now applied to Jesus.

What does all of this mean? It means that John and the Jews expected that the Messiah would surely come from the line of David.

Think about this. What did David do as king of Israel? He established a religious and political order, formed an army, went to war and conquered all of Israel's enemies. He led the nation in the worship of Yahweh. He established the Davidic kingdom and made Israel the ruling nation through his military might and leadership.

Can you see it? With an expectation that the Messiah would come through the line of David also came the expectation He would be a king in the manner of David. He would conquer the pagans and subject all nations under the rule of the one true God. He would reinstate Israel's preeminence as God's chosen people.[6] He would lead Israel back to pure and holy worship, and He would rescue Israel from all religious and sociopolitical enemies.[7]

John Expected a Prophet Like Moses

Preparing the way of the Lord, as prophesied by Isaiah, was understood as the precursor to the imminent manifestation of the Messiah. As scholar J. Jeremias explains,

> When John, on the basis of Is. 40:3, arose in the wilderness, according to the thinking of the age this was an indication that the Messiah, as the second Moses, would manifest Himself in the wilderness. That this was the thinking of the Baptist himself is

very likely, since his baptism was a counterpart to the washing which Moses made the wilderness generation undergo before receiving salvation.[8]

After wandering in the desert for forty years, Moses began to prepare his people to go into the Promised Land. He reviewed the law, and he prophesied that God would one day raise up a prophet who would function as he did, and to whom they were to listen as if they were listening to God (see Deuteronomy 18:15). This prophet would have the commands of Yahweh in his mouth.

When John began baptizing and declaring that the Kingdom of heaven was at hand, he was asked whether he was the anointed one (the Christ), Elijah or the prophet (see Luke 3:15; John 1:21). Not just any prophet, but *the* prophet, alluding to the coming prophet who would be like Moses. Remember, Moses had been a prophet, a lawgiver and Israel's most cherished deliverer who brought them out from slavery and bondage to Egypt. In other words, the expected Messiah was to be a prophet as Moses had been. They believed not only that He would speak the words of the Lord, but also that He would bring the laws of God to bear on religious corruption. He would bring deliverance from sociopolitical oppression.

The Christ, the Prophet or Elijah

In the question about whether John was the Christ, the prophet or Elijah, the Messianic expectations of the people (and John, himself) are revealed. The title of *Christ* means "the anointed one," implying the Messiah. The Christ would be the Son of man and from the line of David. *The prophet* is a reference to the one like Moses (see Deuteronomy 18:15; John 1:25, 45). These are the most common Messianic expectations of this time. Still, there were some who expected an Elijah figure who

34

would be a powerful, fiery prophet who would confront false prophets, idolatry, apostasy and corrupt leaders.

Perhaps you can now understand the magnitude of John's expectations when he declared publicly, "This was he of whom I said, 'He who comes after me ranks before me'" (John 1:15). John, as well as all of Israel at the time, expected Jesus to be a king who would take up arms and deliver Israel forcefully from its servitude to Rome. They believed He would remove all political and cultural oppression from Caesar, and He would expose all the religious corruption of Herod, the Pharisees and the Sadducees. They believed that they would be rescued and restored to their rightful place.

Is There Going to Be a Revolution?

What is the point of reviewing Messianic figures and expectations? John is expecting not just someone to bring revival but a revolutionary who will violently overthrow the political, religious and cultural systems of the day. He believed that the Messiah would lead a righteous rebellion that was backed by God.

Yet where was John presently? He was shackled cruelly in prison suffering violence at the hands of the unrighteous and idolatrous Herod. What was Jesus doing about it? Not a thing. *Is there going to be a revolution?* John wondered. Yes, John, of another kind.

Summary Points

1. The Kingdom of God suffers violence. It has been the way of the Kingdom since the beginning and will continue to be. Jesus warned us it would be so.

2. John the Baptist identified Jesus as the One who was coming to baptize with the Holy Spirit and fire. He said that the Messiah would take away the sins of the world. And yet he asks the strange question, "Are you the One who is coming, or are we to look for another?"

3. The question John asked Jesus involved the Messianic expectations of Israel in his time.

4. John knew he was not the Christ. He knew that he was the one who had been sent before the Lord to prepare the way.

5. John, like Israel, expected a Messiah like the Son of man who had been prophesied by Daniel. This Messiah would come from the line of David, and He would be similar to Moses. Each of these expectations embodied a religious zeal and military and political sovereignty that would reform and rescue Israel.

6. John's announcement of the Kingdom of God was a declaration of revolution. The new King and His eternal Kingdom were at hand; therefore, it was urgent that all got their lives right with God, or they would incur His judgment and wrath.

Questions and Activations

1. Set some time aside for reflection. Have a journal and a Bible available. Record your answers, thoughts and anything the Lord says to you during this time.

2. Invite the Holy Spirit to reveal to you the ways in which the culture you live in, the family you grew up in and the schools you were educated in influence your expectations of Jesus. Think and reflect on the church you attended, with its denominational and theological views. Think about your personal experiences, especially those that involve pain and suffering.
3. Answer the questions below.
   • How did each of these experiences shape your understanding of who Jesus is and how He acts in the world?
   • Can you identify your current expectations of Jesus?
   • In what ways have your expectations affected your relationship with Jesus?
   • How do your expectations fit with the biblical revelation of who Jesus is?

Read and Meditate

Luke 4:17–21; John 1:1–29; Acts 2:14–36; Hebrews 1–2; 4:14–16

Exercise

1. Make a list of what each of the passages above reveals about Jesus. Meditate on the items in that list.
2. Below is a list of what Hebrews 1–10 reveals about Jesus. Take some time to read it over. Think about His greatness and majesty. In your worship time, use the list, along with your own list from the exercise above, to declare verbally the praises of our King!

Jesus is the unique Son of God.

God has spoken in these last days through Jesus.

He is the heir of all things.

Through Jesus the universe was created.

Jesus is the radiance, or the shining out, of the glory of God.

Jesus is the exact imprint of the Father's nature.

Jesus upholds the universe by the word of His power.

He made purification of sin on our behalf.

Jesus is seated at the right hand of the Majesty on high.

He is superior to the angels.

Jesus has inherited a name that is more excellent than the angels.

Jesus is the firstborn son of the Father, the begotten Son of God.

The angels worship Jesus.

Jesus' throne is forever and ever.

He is the King of the Kingdom of God.

He possesses a scepter of righteousness.

Jesus loves righteousness.

He hates wickedness.

He has been anointed by the Father with the oil of gladness.

Jesus laid the foundation of the earth in the beginning.

The heavens are the work of His hands.

Though everything created will perish, be worn out and changed, Jesus remains the same forever.

His years will have no end.

All of His enemies will be made a footstool for His feet.

Jesus was made, for a little while, lower than angels. Now He is crowned with glory and honor because of the suffering and death that He tasted for everyone.

Everything is placed in subjection to Him, and nothing will be outside of His control.

Jesus is the founder of our salvation.

He was made perfect through suffering.

Jesus has conquered death and the power of death. He destroyed the works of the devil in order to deliver all who, through the fear of death, were held in slavery.

He was made like His brothers, the offspring of Abraham, in every respect so that He could become a merciful and faithful High Priest for us.

Jesus has made propitiation for our sins.

Jesus suffered when He was tempted; therefore, He is able to help those who are being tempted.

He is greater than Moses.

Jesus is faithful over the house of God.

He is a great High Priest who is able to sympathize with our weaknesses, because He has been tempted in every respect as we are, and yet remained without sin.

Jesus is a priest appointed by God, a forerunner for us, by the power of an indestructible life.

He is the guarantor of a new and better covenant with better promises by His own blood through the Holy Spirit.

He is able to save to the uttermost those who draw near to God through Him.

Jesus lives to make intercession for us.

He offered Himself on our behalf as a sacrifice for sin.

Jesus, by His single offering, has perfected for all time those of us who are being sanctified.

He made a way for us to enter the most holy place, eternally inviting us into the presence of God.

Therefore, since we are surrounded by so great a cloud of witnesses, let us also lay aside every weight, and sin which clings so closely, and let us run with endurance the race that is set before us, looking to Jesus, the founder and perfecter of our faith, who for the joy that was set before him endured the cross, despising the shame, and is seated at the right hand of the throne of God

Hebrews 12:1–2

CHAPTER 2

The Great Temptation

"Go and tell John what you hear and see. . . . And blessed is the one who is not offended by me."

Matthew 11:4, 5

Kimmy, if you ever preach at Angelus Temple, I'll be sitting in the front row cheering you on!" I was astounded. My calling was not only affirmed but supported heartily. No one expected it—least of all me.

When I was a child, my mom remarried. The man she married adopted my sister, brother and me. What we had always known about this dad was that his parents had been faithful Protestants. Dad left the church at about the age of fifteen, although he and mom attended occasionally the Southern Baptist church around the corner from where I grew up.

On this evening, my family had gathered so that I could tell them of my radical encounter with the Holy Spirit. What were they going to say? Yes, I spoke in tongues. Yes, I had been slain in the Spirit. Yes, I had heard God's voice call me into a full-time ministry that would include preaching, speaking and prophesying to the world. Yes, I would become part of the Pentecostal charismatic movement and a member of the International Church of the Foursquare Gospel.

I had no idea how they would react. My mom, dad and siblings were Southern Baptist. I had not been raised to believe in the supernatural. In a surprising revelation, however, my whole family heard something we had never heard before.

My dad told us how his parents had participated in Pentecostalism. In fact, even while they were deacons at a mainline evangelical church, they regularly attended services at Angelus Temple. They had believed in divine healing and spoke in tongues. As a young man, my dad had attended healing services that had been led by famed healing evangelist and founder of the Foursquare Church, Sister Aimee Semple McPherson. When he finished his story, he made the affirming declaration above.

While my three-year-old self could never have understood why she had been allowed to experience the suffering of watching her biological father leave, as an adult I realized that in my new situation, I was set up for success. I had been adopted by a man whose parents were Foursquare in practice, who had sat under the ministry of Sister Aimee and who had received the infilling of the Spirit with the gift of tongues. My father not only approves of my work, but he is one of my greatest cheerleaders. God knew. He saw what was to be part of my future, and He brought a man to father me who would create my heritage and inheritance.

In Isaiah we read, "For my thoughts are not your thoughts, neither are your ways my ways, declares the LORD. For as the heavens are higher than the earth, so are my ways higher than your ways and my thoughts than your thoughts" (Isaiah 55:8–9). Sometimes the ways of our omniscient, omnipotent and sovereign God are far beyond our ability to think or imagine.

Sometimes, as we live out various seasons and circumstances like the pieces of a puzzle, we are not aware of the bigger picture that is being fit together by God.

John Did Not Understand

John the Baptist was in prison. He was suffering cruel punishment at the hands of an unrighteous, idolatrous and religiously and politically corrupt "King of the Jews." Herod was a Roman pawn in the hands of Caesar.

The last we heard from John was his question to Jesus. After everything he had proclaimed fiercely and prophetically about the Kingdom, the Lamb of God, the coming baptism of the Holy Spirit and fire, and how Jesus was the One, he now seems confused, or at least in need of confirmation.

John was expecting a revolution that would have political, religious and cultural consequences. If Jesus was the one who was coming, would He not be setting up His Kingdom, taking action to overthrow the sociopolitical oppressors, calling for a reformation among the religious elite and establishing Himself as the righteous, divinely appointed King? Would He not be intervening in John's prison situation, since He would be bringing His fiery judgment to bear on all iniquity? According to John's expectations, the answer would have been yes. Yet Jesus was not lifting His voice or a finger to defend and deliver John.

Does it seem farfetched to say that John was struggling? Jesus said John was the Elijah to come. What we know about Elijah is that he was a man with a nature as ours. This means he was not without human weaknesses and struggles (see James 5:17). As Elijah was human, so was John. In his moment of doubt, he sent his disciples to Jesus with the question that was laced with subtle accusation. Are You the One?

Jesus responded to John's question.

"Go and tell John what you hear and see: the blind receive their sight and the lame walk, lepers are cleansed and the deaf hear, and the dead are raised up, and the poor have good news preached to them. *And blessed is the one who is not offended by me.*"

Matthew 11:4–6, emphasis added

Jesus replied without gall or reproach. He gave a list of His current activities and finished with something that at first glance seems curious. Let's not miss it.

He said the one who does not get offended by Him is blessed. Jesus has answered John's subtle accusation with a challenge and a warning. I believe that this warning is not just for John, but for all who are within hearing in every age. Essentially, Jesus has diagnosed John's struggle: John is in danger of becoming offended.

The Temptation

The word Jesus uses to diagnose John's condition is *skandalízō*, or in English "scandalized."[1] At this juncture, we need to have a short lesson in Greek in order to understand fully the significance of what is happening. Originally, this word was used to describe a piece of wood that was used to hold open a trap. When the piece of wood is tripped by an animal, the trap snaps shut, and the animal is stuck. The word was used to mean entrapment.

In the New Testament, the meaning is modified in such a way that it can suggest an obstacle or a stumbling stone that may cause a person to fall into sin. It can cause someone to fall away from the truth or to turn away from his or her faith and become an apostate. Though the meaning is modified, it retains the sense of entrapment by way of enticement or temptation.[2] Putting it all together, when a person is offended, they are being enticed or tempted to unbelief. It is a trap.

The apostle Paul tells us that unbelief will cause us to waver concerning the promises of God (see Romans 4:20). John was being tempted to unbelief. Jesus challenged John not to allow offense to take root and cause him to stumble and fall away. He was in danger of rejecting Jesus, the very One he was sent to prepare the way for. Shocking! Scandalous! Before we judge John, however, let's think about his situation.

Had John not been on God's assignment? Had he not been obedient to everything the Lord had asked of him? Had he not followed God with all of his heart, mind, soul and strength? Had he not announced the Kingdom of heaven and denounced all sin, idolatry and rebellion toward God? Had he not embraced Jesus fully and freely? Had he not even given Jesus his own disciples? Yes! Now he was imprisoned. What for? For announcing the coming revolution, for standing in his prophetic office and for calling out the sin of Israel's leader.

John was suffering unjustly. He was being tempted to unbelief because of his suffering, and he was in danger of becoming offended at Jesus because of his circumstances. John expected a Messiah who would start a revolution. Jesus was scandalizing John's understanding of what that revolution would look like and what the result would be for himself and for Israel. His unmet expectations opened a door to offense, which was the temptation to unbelief that would cause him to sin by rejecting Jesus.

Offended at God

For John there would be no deliverance. Jesus knew it. Still, He warned John not to be offended. John would have to choose whether or not he would believe without the promise of rescue. John would have to make a decision without receiving the confirmation, explanation or revelation that he had expected. He would have to resist temptation and choose to believe even in the face of insult, injustice and injury. The scandalizing of his expectations left him confused, skeptical and tempted toward unbelief. In that experience and those circumstances, Jesus called him to faith.

Just this week, I read of another worship leader who renounced publicly his faith in God. He is no longer a Christian. What was his reason? He became offended. He asked how a just God could allow injustice. How could a loving God send people to hell? How could a kind God allow people to suffer the horrors of sickness and evil? He mentioned that he had always been aghast at the Old Testament stories of whole cities and families being wiped out at God's command. He became offended at God, and he no longer believes.

Over my years of pastoring, I have counseled many who had become offended at God because of a terrible injustice, a hurtful betrayal or a loved one who had suffered and died a violent death. How often do we, when we have unmet expectations or when we begin to feel the sharp edge of opposition and injustice, become offended with God? We begin to doubt His love, His goodness, His faithfulness, His presence and even His reality. How many have turned back and no longer follow Jesus because of this very thing?

We expected to be treated differently. We expected a circumstance to end differently. We expected God to come through—after all, we believed Him. Can you hear what is happening here? We become the judge who is putting God on trial. We hold God responsible and accountable for our pain and suffering. We hold up our wounds and scars, our failed agendas and unmet expectations, and ask Him to explain Himself. C. S. Lewis, in his essay, "God in the Dock," described it this way:

> The ancient man approached God (or even the gods) as the accused person approaches his judge. For the modern man, the roles are quite reversed. He is the judge: God is in the dock. He

46

is quite a kindly judge; if God should have a reasonable defense for being the god who permits war, poverty, and disease, he is ready to listen to it. The trial may even end in God's acquittal. But the important thing is that man is on the bench and God is in the dock.[3]

We judge God because we are offended by Him. We are offended that He did not do what we expected Him to do. In our judgments, Jesus comes and says to us what he said to John: "Blessed is the one who is not offended by me" (Matthew 11:6).

Offense and a Move of God

John was the forerunner for a move of God—the inauguration of the Kingdom of God. He had the privilege of preparing the way before Jesus, the King of this new Kingdom. As he is experiencing the intimidation and violence stirred by the announcement of the coming Kingdom, however, he is tempted to shrink back from his faith in Jesus.

Remember, the temptation to unbelief is a trap. It is a block to faith, and it is a roadblock to moving forward with God. When we become offended with God, we misunderstand or distrust Him and what He is doing. When we are offended at God, we will sacrifice our opportunity to join Him where He is working. This is exactly where the enemy wants us: offended and sidelined. It is the scheme of the devil to get us to sit down, cross our arms over our chest and sit out a move of God.

This is how the enemy kills a movement of the Spirit. People, even influential leaders, become trapped in offense. They become offended at any number of things, including who God chooses to lead, unpredictable manifestations of His presence, or one another. They began with a different expectation of how things would go, how it would look and how they would be used. Their disappointment becomes a stumbling stone over which they fall and turn away. They reject the movement. They reject the possibility that a move of God can come through hippies, Catholics, the poor, immigrants or women. They reject such possibilities because their particular pet doctrines or denominations are challenged rather than embraced. They refuse to believe that God is the author of the movement, and they begin to denounce, criticize or find fault publicly. The enemy seizes the opportunity to cause violent division, opposition and persecution.

Revival history is filled with stories of opposition toward a move of God and of His people being persecuted. The Great Awakenings, camp revivals, Pentecostalism, the charismatic and the Renewal movements all had vitriolic opponents claiming heresy, fraud and illegitimacy. Though not without some problematic issues, the results of these moves of God included sweeping salvations, fantastic works of mercy and social reform. The fruit is undeniable.

We are on the precipice of another great move of God; therefore, we will be scandalized in some way. If we want to walk in the way of the Kingdom and join God in a move of the Spirit in our generation, we need to be unoffendable.

According to Scripture, facing offense is inevitable. Jesus said offenses must come (see Matthew 18:7). We will experience violence in some form as the Kingdom of God advances and the Spirit moves. We will all be confronted with the temptation not to believe. In that moment, we will each have the opportunity to decide whether or not we will resist the unbelief we feel in the face of insult, injustice and injury.

If we let Him, God will scandalize our expectations so that He can shift the narrative of our lives and do something new. A seminary professor of mine used to say that every breakthrough begins with a breakdown. I like to say that if nothing changes, nothing changes. Change, like offense, is inevitable.

Change requires a scandalizing of what we thought we understood about someone or something. It causes a breakdown of what we thought we knew in order to get a breakthrough into what we do not know. When we experience change in our expectations, we can become freed from attitudes, emotions, mind-sets or world views in which we have become stuck.

Jesus was scandalizing John's expectation of the Messiah that he built on national and cultural expectations extrapolated from Scripture. He was not punishing John. He was warning John not to stay stuck through offense and end up missing the breakthrough. He was challenging John's world view and mind-set in order to bring him a Kingdom perspective. We will develop this more in the coming chapters. For now, we have an opportunity to get right with God and move forward.

Dealing with Offense

Being offended is a choice. "Blessed is the one who is not offended by me" means we can choose. We can decide not to give in to the thoughts and emotions the enemy uses to tempt us to become offended. We can choose to repent from all offense toward God and toward people. We can refuse to take the place of judge and jury. We can give that place back to its rightful owner—our Lord, the Creator and Sustainer of all things. We can choose to believe what God said through the prophet Isaiah when he told us that His ways are not our ways, and His thoughts are not our thoughts (see Isaiah 55:8). He thinks and acts in ways we do not, cannot and will not, because He is far beyond us. This is the first step in becoming unoffendable.

The second is to examine our expectations and offer them to the Lord to scandalize in any way He desires. Let's ask ourselves where we have been tempted to step into unbelief because God or people have not fulfilled our expectations or rescued us from our suffering. Where have we become convinced

49

that we do not need Jesus and His saving grace? Where do we believe we have suffered unjustly or feel that we deserve exoneration, remuneration, vengeance or rescue?

If we will answer these questions honestly and transparently, with the help of the Spirit of God who searches the heart and mind, we can discover where we have become offended and trapped. We can be rescued from the grip of temptation and the trap of Satan. In this way, we will be open again to hear and obey the voice of God. We will be prepared to walk in the way of the Kingdom and to participate in a mighty move of God, whatever may come. Let's pray, shall we?

Prayer of Repentance

Father, forgive me. Forgive me for all of the times that I have required You, Your people or Your ways to fulfill my expectations, my traditions or my guidelines. Forgive me for requiring You and others You have placed in my life to do only what is in my comfort zone, according to my concept of what is ordered and decent. Father, anytime I criticized or judged a manifestation of the Spirit because it did not look like what I deemed to be spiritual or acceptable, forgive me. Anytime I was scandalized or offended by a word spoken or an action taken because it cost me something, it caused suffering or it was a perceived injustice, forgive me. Father, wherever I have stood in judgement of You and Your ways by questioning Your motives, distrusting Your heart or demanding that You give an account of Your actions, forgive me. I choose by an act of my will to come out of agreement with any spirit of unbelief, criticism, judgment, religion, political partisanship, false expectation or disappointment because of circumstances and situations where I had expectations of You, the Church, leaders, friends or family that was not met. I forgive them. I humble myself and declare that You alone are God. Jesus Christ, the Son of God, is my Savior and my Lord. In His name, the powerful unmatched name of Jesus, I take authority over and break the power of every spirit of offense, every religious spirit and all false expectations. I command you, in the name of Jesus, to now go! All of your maneuvers, schemes and tactics are now made null and void in my life. Father, I ask You to heal me. Heal my broken heart. Heal and restore my wounded soul. I invite You to come and do whatever You want to do in and through my life. Holy Spirit, come fill me afresh, give me ears to hear and the power to obey. Thank You. In Jesus' name, Amen.

Summary Points

1. John had been expecting a revolution with political, religious and cultural consequences. He found himself, instead, in prison suffering violence unjustly at the hands of Herod. His suffering caused him to struggle and question whether or not Jesus was the Messiah.

2. John, with subtle accusation, sends his disciples to ask Jesus, "Are You the One?"

3. Jesus responds to John's question with a testimony of His supernatural work. He references Isaiah 29:18 and Isaiah 35:5–6, inferring He is doing the work of the Messiah.

4. Jesus warns John and all within hearing to guard against being offended, being scandalized or becoming entrapped. In the New Testament, the meaning of *offense* is modified in such a way that it can suggest an obstacle or stumbling stone that may cause a person to fall into sin, to fall away from the truth or to become an apostate and turn away from faith.

5. When a person is offended, they are being enticed or tempted to unbelief. It is a trap.

6. Jesus challenges John to be careful not to allow himself to be offended. Jesus knew that John was in danger of rejecting Him, the very One he was sent to prepare the way for.

7. John's expectations of the revolution that the Messiah would initiate for both him and Israel were being scandalized. His unmet expectations opened a door to offense and the temptation to unbelief. John would have to resist temptation and choose to believe even in the face of insult, injustice and injury.

8. When we have unmet expectations or when we experience opposition and injustice, we often become offended. In these circumstances, we direct our offense toward God. We doubt His love, His goodness, His faithfulness, His presence and even His reality. We put God on trial and become His judge. We hold God responsible and ask Him to explain Himself.

9. The enemy can kill a movement of the Spirit when people become trapped in offense. The enemy seizes opportunities to cause violent division, opposition and persecution. Revival history is filled with moves of God being opposed and those who are involved being persecuted. The Great Awakenings, camp revivals, Pentecostalism and the charismatic and Renewal movements all had vitriolic opponents claiming heresy, fraud and illegitimacy.

10. We are on the precipice of another great move of God. If we want to walk in the way of the Kingdom and join God in a move of the Spirit in our generation, we need to be unoffendable. According to Scripture, facing offense is inevitable. Jesus said to expect it.

11. Being offended is a choice. We can decide now not to give in to the thoughts and emotions the enemy will use to tempt us to become offended. We can choose to repent from all offense toward God and toward people. We can refuse to be judge and jury and give that place back to its rightful owner—the Lord. We can choose to believe that God is good all of the time.

Questions and Activation

1. Set some time aside for reflection. Have a journal and a Bible available. Record your answers, thoughts and anything the Lord says to you during this time.

2. Invite the Holy Spirit into your reflection time. Think and reflect on the expectations you identified in chapter 1. Think and reflect on any unmet expectations of Jesus and of His being present for you in your life in relation to work, finances, family, relationships or ministry. Think and reflect on the times that you felt let down, betrayed or ignored by God.

3. Answer the questions below.

   - Have I built a wall that separates me from God?

   - Have I required certain actions or behaviors of God or others toward me?

   - Have I believed the lie that I have been betrayed by God?

   - Do I hold the Lord responsible for my unmet expectations?

   - How have my unmet expectations affected my view of Jesus or my relationship with Him?

   - Where have I been tempted toward unbelief because God or His people have not fulfilled my expectations or rescued me from my suffering?

   - Where have I become convinced that I do not need Jesus or His saving grace?

   - Where have I suffered unjustly or feel that I am justified in my offense deserving exoneration, remuneration, vengeance and rescue?

Read and Meditate

Isaiah 52:7–53:12

Exercise

1. Invite the Holy Spirit to heal and cleanse you from all offense.

2. Repent from offenses revealed through the questions above and the Scripture passage in Isaiah. Ask the Lord to forgive, cleanse and renew you for

   - walls that you built out of fear and self-protection.
   - the pride of requiring Him to act according to your specifications.
   - believing lies sent by the enemy about Him.
   - holding Him responsible for _____ [name your unmet expectations].
   - unresolved anger or bitterness over the unmet expectations.
   - allowing yourself to entertain or agree with indignation and self-righteousness that has led to the rejection of Jesus in any way.

Repentance is a gift from God. Paul wrote, "Do not be conformed to this world, but be transformed by the renewal of your mind, that by testing you may discern what is the will of God, what is good and acceptable and perfect" (Romans 12:2). It is part of the work of the Holy Spirit to transform us and help our minds be renewed so that we may know and live out the good, acceptable and perfect will of God. As we yield to the Spirit's work of transforming and cleansing our hearts, we can change our minds and go in a new direction. We can live as new creatures in Christ Jesus, abiding in Him, bearing good fruit and saying with Paul, "The life I now live in the flesh I live by faith in the Son of God, who loved me and gave himself for me" (Galatians 2:20).

Pray

Father, in the name of Jesus I choose not to agree with the lie that You have betrayed me, left me, ignored my cry or treated me unjustly. I no longer allow myself to believe that You are unloving, unkind or unjust. I come out of alignment and agreement with a spirit of pride, fear, bitterness, resentment or offense. I reject the attitudes, thoughts, emotions and perspectives that have accompanied these lies. I take authority over any deception, lies or demonic bondage that were brought upon me when I opened a door to them through my sin of offense. I break their power now, in Jesus' name. I invite You, Holy Spirit, to cleanse and fill me. In Jesus' name, Amen.

Declare Truth

I declare and decree that

- I will no longer be deceived into believing lies about God. I declare that He is good, kind, loving, just, merciful, faithful, forgiving and covenant keeping. He will not abandon me. He does not lie, and there is nothing that can snatch me out of His hand.
- I will not give in to unbelief when I experience suffering or injustice. I will trust in God who sees me, is with

me always and is working everything together for good in my life according to His will and purpose.

- I will no longer be tossed about by every wind and wave of adversity, but I will be steadfast and look to Jesus. He is my rock and my refuge.
- I will choose the narrow way of faith and remain humble in my walk with the Lord.

CHAPTER 3

Ears to Hear

And Jesus answered them, "Go and tell John what you hear and see: the blind receive their sight and the lame walk, lepers are cleansed and the deaf hear, and the dead are raised up, and the poor have good news preached to them."

Matthew 11:4–5

The roar in the room was deafening. All of the pastors and leaders were standing with their arms raised high. As I made my way through each row of the large church sanctuary, they were calling out praises to the Lord as they were awaiting their turn to receive prayer by the laying on of hands. They were expecting a fresh touch of the Holy Spirit and a personal prophetic word as I ministered to them. The people who had come from various churches around the city to attend the healing meeting were seated, praying in tongues with great conviction.

A small group had formed in the front with a young man in the center. His whole body shook, and his surprised expression communicated that he did not know exactly what was happening to him. He did not, however, resist the process, because it was apparent that God was at work supernaturally in his physical body. The audience began to rise in anticipation.

He had arrived without much notice. In the poor neighborhoods of this nation, a person who gets around by using metal crutches to drag his legs along is nothing noteworthy. Nine months earlier, he had been in a car accident. This trauma had stolen his ability to ambulate. The accident damaged his spine and devastated his dreams. He was barely out of his teens.

The supernatural power of the Spirit filled the young man, which caused his body to shake and to be filled with strength that was not his own. There was a supernatural energy that was supplied by the Holy Spirit that seemed to lift him into a standing position.

Those who knew him began to cry aloud and reach out to support his tentative stance. He stood for minutes, which seemed like hours, trembling, weeping and praying in tongues. With Herculean effort, he slid a limp leg forward. One step. One miraculous feat. Then another, and another. Abruptly, it seemed to end. He stood in front of me without moving.

I sensed that the Holy Spirit was not finished, so I laid hands on him and commanded healing in his body. Another burst of energy came upon him. His legs began to twitch, then jerk, then jump. They seemed possessed with a life of their own as if they were detached from the rest of his body. The look on his face was a mix of terror and wonder. Suddenly, he was jumping up and down wildly as his friends and the pastors linked arms together to create a safe human corral.

The time of prayer for him lasted nearly fifteen minutes. In the end, he held his metal crutches over his head as he ran a victory lap around the platform. The church erupted in praise, and his parents wept in gratitude. He was healed. The Kingdom of God was at hand.

Let me tell you another story from an incredible healing meeting in another country. A beautiful young woman who had been deaf in one of her ears since birth asked me to pray for her. She seemed shocked, confused, joyful, tearful and amazed when her ear had popped open as I had laid hands on her and prayed for healing. She had been pressured by her friends to ask me for prayer. She had been reluctant to do so, however, because she had asked many others, many times before without result. Not this time. This time, the Kingdom of God was made manifest in her healing. Undoubtedly, the Kingdom of God had come near.

When I asked her what happened, she replied with a giggle and halting speech. "I . . . I don't know. All . . . all I know . . . is that I could not hear and now I can!"

The Answer

For two chapters, we have focused on John and his strange question. As unpredictable as John's question is, Jesus' answer appears even more so.

"Are you the one who is to come, or shall we look for another?" (Matthew 11:3). This is a closed-ended question. Jesus could have simply said, "Yes, John, I am," but He does not. Why? What is He trying to tell John, John's disciples, the crowds and the readers of this passage?

Jesus is making a point. He is changing the narrative. Remember, Jesus is challenging John's world view and mind-set in order to help him receive a Kingdom perspective. In fact, there are three comments Jesus makes that mark this passage.

He tells John's disciples to "Go and tell John what you hear and see" (Matthew 11:4). He chides the crowds saying, "He who has ears to hear, let him hear" (Matthew 11:15). Then he warns (or insults) the religious leaders saying that wisdom is justified by her deeds, which implies that they are not (see Matthew 11:19).

In these verses, God is scandalizing everyone's notion of the coming Messianic Kingdom, be it John, the crowd or the religious leaders.

Go and Tell John

Recall that John's understanding of the coming Messiah was apocalyptic. He was anticipating a winnowing and separating of the wheat and chaff of human political and religious oppression. These expectations resembled the prophecies of Daniel in which corrupt human institutions and governments were toppled by righteous, fiery judgement. Jesus knows John is asking if He is the Messiah. He also knows John's expectations. Jesus tells John's disciples to open their eyes and ears to *see and hear* what is happening—something different, something new and something mysterious. The Kingdom has come.

Jesus sends an answer to John regarding the works He is doing that can be seen by all but that need to be understood. He gives a specified and strategic list of His current activities. He has performed many miracles, and His works give witness to His anointing and His teaching. He sends word that the blind see, the lame walk, the lepers are cleansed, the deaf hear, the dead are raised and the poor have good news preached to them. The list He sends is the message. It is the message of the new era. The Kingdom of God and its King are here.

The list is an allusion, or an implied reference to a person, event or thing that is based on the assumption that there is a body of knowledge that is shared by the author and the reader. This shared knowledge allows the reader to understand the author's reference.[1] Jesus is pointing intentionally to something specific by listing these particular activities. The list is a reference to a prophecy that tells what will take place when God returns and saves His people.

"Behold, your God will come with vengeance, with the recompense of God. He will come and save you." *Then the eyes of the blind shall be opened, and the ears of the deaf unstopped; then shall the lame man leap like a deer, and the tongue of the mute sing for joy.*

Isaiah 35:4–6, emphasis added

It is also a reference to Jesus as the Spirit-anointed King, the Christ, who is setting the captives free. Luke records the moment when Jesus—after being baptized by John, being anointed by the Spirit of God and overcoming the temptation of Satan in the wilderness—goes into the temple and reads from Isaiah.

"The Spirit of the Lord is upon me, because he has anointed me to proclaim good news to the poor. He has sent me to proclaim liberty to the captives and recovering of sight to the blind, to set at liberty those who are oppressed, to proclaim the year of the Lord's favor." . . . And he began to say to them, "*Today this Scripture has been fulfilled in your hearing.*"

Luke 4:18–21, emphasis added

The answer Jesus sent to John was a new perspective on the fulfillment of the Messianic hope. Yes, John, Jesus is the King, and the Kingdom has come. He is the God who saves. Healing, deliverance and life are the demonstrations of the Gospel, and the Gospel is good news to all who are impoverished in soul and who are living in darkness. Those who have ears to hear will work out the veiled message and will accept the new narrative.

He Who Has Ears

Ears to hear were especially important in Jesus' time. Israel was a culture that practiced oral transmission as its method of passing down its history, Scripture and traditions to each generation. In addition, the God of Israel is a God who speaks. God spoke in many ways and at many times by the prophets (see Hebrews 1:1). Scripture also says that God spoke by His Son, Jesus (see Hebrews 1:2). From the beginning, God desired a people who would hear His voice and live by every word that came from His mouth (see Matthew 4:4).

When He speaks, it is time to listen and understand (see Job 36:10; Isaiah 50:5; John 10:27; Matthew 13:1–23). The Bible tells us that hearing is related to faith and faithfulness. Ears to hear is an idiomatic saying that calls for the listener to have an open heart and mind to what is about to be revealed. In other words, saying, "He who has ears to hear, let him hear" is the same thing as saying, "Wake up, and pay careful attention!" Thus, Jesus is instructing the crowds that what He is saying is significant and is revelation from God, so they had better listen in order to understand something new.

Jesus is revealing the way of the Kingdom. Remember, John is not the only one whose expectations regarding the Messianic revolution are being scandalized. N. T. Wright describes the Jews' idea of the Kingdom:

Their vision of the kingdom was all about revolution. Swords, spears, surprise attacks; some hurt, some killed, winning in the end. Violence to defeat violence. A holy war against the unholy warriors. Love your neighbor, hate your enemy; if he slaps you on the cheek, or makes you walk a mile with him, stab him with his own dagger. That's the sort of kingdom-vision they had. And Jesus could see, with the clarity both of the prophet and of sheer common sense, where it would lead. Better to be in Sodom and Gomorrah, with fire and brimstone raining from heaven, than fighting God's battles with the devil's weapons. He was offering a last chance to embrace a different kingdom-vision. He'd outlined it in his great sermon and the teaching he was giving in towns and villages all over Galilee. He was living it out on the street, and in houses filled with laughter and friendship. He was showing how powerful it was with his healings.[2]

If the people will have ears to hear, they will also have the opportunity to participate in a great move of God.

Wisdom's Children

What was the revelation about which the crowds needed to have ears to hear? It was that the inbreaking Kingdom of God was not the expected military revolution in which all corrupt people, leaders and institutions would be punished. It was going to be a Spirit-empowered spiritual revolution. It would grow like leaven in a batch of flour, it would touch every sphere of humanity and it would change everything. This revolution would establish the rule and reign of God and would shine light in every dark place. Not even death, loss of possession and property, imprisonment, or violence would be able stop the move of the Holy Spirit and His ultimate victory.

Yet only spiritual perception can understand spiritual revelation. Those without ears to hear will become offended. Jesus indicts the people and their religious leaders saying,

> "But to what shall I liken this generation? It is like children sitting in the marketplaces and calling to their companions, and saying: 'We played the flute for you, and you did not dance; we mourned to you, and you did not lament.' For John came neither eating nor drinking, and they say, 'He has a demon.' The Son of Man came eating and drinking, and they say, 'Look, a glutton and a winebibber, a friend of tax collectors and sinners!' But wisdom is justified by her children."
>
> Matthew 11:16–19 NKJV

In simple language, if we get stuck in our position and expectations, we become partisans who listen defensively, who become offended and who reject rather than hear. Once we reject, we refuse repentance. Once we refuse repentance, the narrow way to be able to receive the Kingdom is closed.

How many have missed a move of God because they engaged in defensive communication and could not perceive what God was doing? They recused themselves rather than opening their hearts and minds. They insulted, criticized and defended their positions rather than change. We live in a time when God is moving. Everything is shifting and shaking around us.

In November 2016, on the day Donald Trump was elected president, I heard the Lord say, *If you knew that you had only four years to do business freely, what would you set in place now?* I was surprised by this question and did not have a ready answer. I knew I would need a special kind of wisdom to know what to do. I also knew the Lord was arresting my attention in order to give me revelation for the challenging times that may lie ahead. I began to watch and listen. What began to unfold was a message about being shrewd in seasons of change, crisis and challenge.

Soon after hearing the question above, I saw a movie called *Hidden Figures*. This movie tells the story of Katherine G. Johnson, Dorothy Vaughan and Mary Jackson. In the 1960s, during a time in America of great change, racial division, turmoil and transition, these Black, marginalized women managed to see beyond the resistance and limits that had been placed on them. They stepped into an opportunity no one else saw. As I watched, I knew this was part of the revelation God was bringing to me. I understood that the characters in the movie were acting as wisdom's children. They were shrewd.

Jesus tells a story of a man who is threatened with economic crisis (see Luke 16:1–8). He allows adversity to stimulate creative strategies to thrive in the midst of great change. He sees the reset coming and uses the resources and position available to him to take advantage of the situation. Jesus then illuminates us saying, "For the sons of this world are more shrewd in dealing with their own generation than the sons of light" (Luke 16:8).

It is time for us to be wisdom's children. It is time for us to be sons of light who are shrewd and who have ears to hear. We cannot serve the culture and politics and still be able to take our place in the Kingdom. The shifts, sudden changes and even crises can both create unprecedented opportunities for Kingdom advancement and stimulate creative Kingdom strategies for finance, business, politics, family, education and ministry.

Shrewd in Our Generation

What does it mean to be shrewd? *Shrewdness* in Scripture means to have a combination of wisdom, understanding and revelatory knowledge. It involves critical judgment with prophetic insight and foresight. Isaiah compares those who bow down to a block of wood to those who are not shrewd (see Isaiah 44:17). Can a block of wood be a god simply because it is carved into a shape? In contemporary terms, can my 5,000 Facebook friends give me true community? The answer to both questions is no. To believe so would not be shrewd.

Shrewdness is what Paul assumes we all have when he says, "I speak as to wise [shrewd] men, judge for yourselves what I say" (1 Corinthians 10:15 NKJV). The word used for *wise* in this passage is the same Greek word that is translated "shrewd" in Luke 16.

If we are shrewd, we do not judge hearts. Rather, we judge situations, policies and philosophies and the fruit that people produce in their lives. Shrewdness is what Jesus expects of His disciples when He says, "Behold, I am sending you out as sheep in the midst of wolves; so be as shrewd as serpents, and as innocent as doves" (Matthew 10:16 NASB1995).

You see, there is a mission. We are all are being sent out to gather the harvest and expand the Kingdom (see Matthew 9:37; John 4). The mission takes place in a hostile world where the Kingdom of God suffers violence. In this kind of world, we are to be shrewd as serpents and innocent as doves.

Why a serpent? To understand this, we must take a look at the first serpent—the one in the Garden of Eden. Genesis describes that serpent as crafty, the most cunning beast created (see Genesis 3:1). In other words, the serpent was shrewd. He saw the big picture, and he acted in order to redirect the outcome.

The serpent understood that man was made in God's image and had been given dominion over everything. He was after that dominion. He had come against God and had been thrown to the earth (see Revelation 12:7–9). Now he would come against God's image and against humanity in order to take dominion over God's creation. His ultimate goal was to become lord of the age. He was shrewd.

We are charged by Jesus to be as shrewd as a serpent and to see the big picture. This means we are to see and assess what is happening presently, as well as what will come in the future. If we do, we will be able to redirect the outcome on behalf of the Kingdom. If only Adam and Eve had been shrewd in the Garden. Even still, Jesus has taken back what was lost, and He gives it to us once more. Will we be shrewd?

Will we be not only shrewd but also innocent? Paul warns us to be shrewd as to what is good, but innocent as to what is the work of the flesh and darkness (see Romans 6:19). Why? Because without being led by the Holy Spirit in submission to God's will and mission, and without having the right heart and pure motives, shrewdness becomes a snake. We end up acting in manipulative, selfish, self-seeking, underhanded and undermining ways. Yet without shrewdness, innocence is naïve and gullible.

Can you hear what the Spirit is saying? To be shrewd means to have the wisdom and prophetic insight to assess every situation and circumstance in order to act with wisdom, sound judgement and foresight. This behavior will direct the outcome to advance the Kingdom. We are going to encounter hostile situations. We will need to act shrewdly in order to seize the opportunities they afford.

Now is the time for the Body of Christ to awaken to the opportunities that present themselves in the midst of crisis. We must see and hear with new understanding, and we must allow adversity to stimulate creative strategies for advancing the Kingdom. Let's allow the Spirit to scandalize our expectations and narratives so that our world views and mind-sets align with the Kingdom of God for our generation.

Summary Points

1. The response Jesus gives to John's question about whether or not He is the Messiah was an attempt to change the Judaic cultural narrative regarding their Messianic hopes. Jesus challenged John's world view and mind-set in order to bring him a Kingdom of God perspective.

2. The response Jesus gives to John, to the crowd and to all of us is that we must have eyes to see and ears to hear (revelation by the Spirit) in order to discern the coming Kingdom. Understanding the seasons will require a perspective change, and it will mean leaving traditional and cultural expectations behind.

3. The response Jesus gives reveals that He is the Spirit-anointed King, the Christ, who is setting the captives free in fulfillment of Old Testament prophecy (see Isaiah 35:4–5). Healing, deliverance and life is the demonstration of the Gospel of the Kingdom, and it is good news within the new Messianic narrative.

4. The inbreaking Kingdom of God was not the expected military revolution during which all corrupt and sinful people, leaders and institutions would be punished. It was going to be a Spirit-empowered revolution.

5. Wisdom's children are shrewd. Only spiritual perception can understand spiritual revelation. To be shrewd means to have wisdom, understanding and revelatory knowledge.

6. We have a mission given to us by Jesus to gather the harvest and expand the Kingdom. The mission takes place in a hostile world where the Kingdom of God suffers violence. In this kind of world, we are to be shrewd as serpents and innocent as doves.

7. Even in the midst of crisis, the Body of Christ must see and hear with new understanding and allow adversity to stimulate creative strategies for advancing the Kingdom.

Questions and Activation

1. Set some time aside for reflection. Have a journal and a Bible available. Record your answers, thoughts and anything the Lord says to you during this time.

2. Invite the Holy Spirit into your reflection time. Think and reflect on what it means to have ears that hear and eyes that see. Think and reflect on what it means to be shrewd.

   Consider a dream the Lord gave to a friend of mine. In the dream, she walked into her office at work. In her office was an elephant that was dressed up. My friend realized the play on words that was happening as she encountered "a dressed-up elephant."[3] She knew that the Lord was saying to her that it was time to "address the elephant" in the room. The American idiom of an elephant in the room is a refence to an obvious problem no one wants to discuss or challenge.

   My friend could not seem to get breakthrough in her business and finances. The Lord was showing her she would first need to address whatever problem in her life she was avoiding.

3. Answer the questions below.

   • Is there an elephant in your room?

   • Is there anything in your life right now that you are avoiding or that is keeping you blind and deaf to the Spirit?

Read and Meditate

Matthew 7:24–25; Isaiah 60:1–3; Matthew 5:14

Exercise

We need to be people who see with revelational insight the things that need to be set in place in order to secure the future. We want to join the Spirit as He advances the Kingdom in our finances, businesses, families, callings, health and attitudes. Facing adversity will stir up creativity for Kingdom strategies. The Kingdom of God will be advanced in our lives and in the lives around us. We will be positioned to be used by God in our neighborhoods, cities, nations and the world.

Read this aloud as a declaration over your life:

As a child of God, I am wisdom's child. A spirit of wisdom is coming upon me *right now*. I declare that the shifts, the crises in my life and the sudden changes are creating unprecedented opportunities for Kingdom advancement. I declare that the shifts in the Church and in my nation are also creating unprecedented opportunities for Kingdom advancement. I declare the adversity will not tear down the Church, discourage the Body or cause us to shrink back; instead, the adversity is stimulating creative Kingdom strategies that are being put in place now and are breaking forth in a new Holy Spirit renaissance. The Body of Christ and I will be the light that is shining. We are the light on the hill. I declare that people and nations will be drawn to our light, and our light will shine in every dark place that exists in our spheres of influence. We will be a people with supernatural wisdom, prophetic insight and foresight, and our mouths will be filled with the powerful Word of God. Light and truth will set free every person who is held in bondage as a slave of darkness. I declare that the blind will see, the deaf will hear, and every sickness and disease will be healed by the blood and the name of Jesus. I have ears to hear and eyes to see what the Spirit is saying and what the Father is doing. I will perceive and participate in the Kingdom of God.

CHAPTER 4

The Least in the Kingdom

"Truly, I say to you, among those born of women there has arisen no one greater than John the Baptist. Yet the one who is least in the kingdom of heaven is greater than he."

Matthew 11:11

"You can't grow if you are afraid of change."

Bernardo Moya

Doctor Kim, please don't read this until I leave," she whispered, stuffing the thick wad of notebook paper into my right hand. I closed my fist around the papers and nodded my head. The beautiful twentysomething woman nearly ran as she left the auditorium. I tucked the mysterious offering in my bag without much consideration and returned to what I had been doing.

The conference had been incredible. The power of the Holy Spirit had manifested in physical healing, inner healing and prophecy. After it wrapped up, I boarded my flight. I was exhausted, but I also had a heart that was filled with gratitude for all that God had done. I was ready to make the long journey across international boundaries toward home. As I lay my head back and closed my eyes, the image of the young woman passed through my mind.

I retrieved the mysterious offering to unfold fifteen handwritten pages that chronicled a life of savage sexual and physical abuse that had begun while she was still a very young child. She had been abused repeatedly by the men in her life—her father, as well as the men her mother had dated or had picked up in bars.

She found Jesus as a teenager, but the abuse continued until she left the house and got married. At the time of the conference, she had several young children, and she was at the end of her rope. Her life was still filled with the pain of her past. She had made the decision that day that there would be no more pain. She had planned to kill herself after work.

God, however, interrupted her plan. He whispered in her ear that He wanted her to go the church conference and listen to the woman from America. It must have taken Herculean strength or supernatural desperation, but she obeyed the Voice. Even still, she was planning on implementing her plan after she returned home from the conference.

I was seated in the front and worship was in progress when the Holy Spirit gave me a prophetic and urgent message. I jumped to my feet and onto the platform, and I breathlessly relayed the message of the Spirit. As a result, weeping and shouting resonated in the auditorium.

Time stopped at that moment for the woman who had planned to kill herself. She wrote that the walls and people fell away, and it seemed as if only she and I were in the room.

My words pierced her armor and drove deep into her heart. She convulsed with pain, fell to the floor and wept uncontrollably for the bulk of the meeting. When the storm passed, she knew that she had been changed.

She realized that the Lord had spared her life, and she knew that she was loved. She knew that she was called. She knew that she could choose life. In the letter, she explained that she knew that she must live and fulfill the purpose for which she was created. She knew that she must live so that her children would grow up and fulfill the purpose for which God had created them. She made the decision that she would believe the Lord and live. Everything would be different from that point on.

A New Era

A few years back, I was struck by the prophetic import of a Cadillac commercial. It announced, "As the season shifts, change is on its way. And with change comes opportunity. It's up to you to seize it."[1] Indeed.

Most people do not like change. It brings up fear of the future, fear of the unknown, fear of not having enough, fear of not knowing enough or fear of not being enough. Viewed through the lens of fear, change looks like loss as opposed to opportunity. Fear distorts vision. Yet the truth is that it is impossible to seize an opportunity that you do not recognize; therefore, in order to seize the opportunity, fear must be resisted.

The author of Hebrews addresses Christians who were living through intense changes. They were afraid and were being tempted to shrink back. He assures them that "they have everything to lose if they fall back, but everything to gain if they press on."[2]

Therefore we must pay much closer attention to what we have heard, lest we drift away from it. For since the message declared

75

by angels proved to be reliable, and every transgression or disobedience received a just retribution, how shall we escape if we neglect such a great salvation? It was declared at first by the Lord, and it was attested to us by those who heard, while God also bore witness by signs and wonders and various miracles and by gifts of the Holy Spirit.

Hebrews 2:1–4, emphasis added

What was this great salvation? What was the message being declared? The King and His Kingdom are here! Signs, wonders and miracles are bearing witness to it all. People are being healed, the dead are being raised and demons are being cast out. God is moving among His people and is changing everything. It is glorious, and it is violent.

We have already seen how Jesus implicates Himself cleverly as the Spirit-anointed King of the Kingdom of God by sending a list of His supernatural activities in a cryptic message for John the Baptist. The message was a revelatory announcement of His true identity for any with ears to hear. It is also a dividing line.

In the beginning of the gospel of Matthew, a baby is born in a stable during a unique stellar event. Wise men from the east interpret the sign in the sky and come looking for the newly birthed, prophesied King of the Jews. The most powerful man in Judea, the self-proclaimed King of the Jews, Herod the Great, sought to assassinate the child-King. Thwarted by the wise men, he ordered the slaughter of all males two years old and under. These were the children of his own people. Why would he go to such an extreme? What could possibly be such a big deal about a baby born in a stable? Herod the Great and his descendants understood that the birth of Christ was a divine political coup that would upend their rule and shift the power base. It is a dividing line.

Jesus is the child who was born. He is the King of all kings, and He brings with Him a divine Kingdom. His Kingdom is not of this world, yet it has come into the world. The son of Herod the Great, Herod Antipas, could not withstand the coming of this Kingdom. He was already overthrown as divine ruler. The Kingdom was being torn from him, and he would forever be nothing more than the Roman lackey who murdered John the Baptist at the behest of a seductress.

What about John? Jesus testifies to the crowds that John is worthy of high honor. He is the prophet who was sent to prepare the way of the Lord. He is the prophesied Elijah who was to point to the reconciliation of God's children through the Messiah. John, however, is also something more. John is the last of his kind. He stands on one side of the dividing line. He is the sign of an end of an era.

Jesus explained, "For all the Prophets and the Law prophesied until John" (Matthew 11:13). No one was greater than John in his era. In the new era, however, even the least will be greater than John. Those who hear and accept the new narrative and who receive the Son, King Jesus, as Lord step across the divide into the new era. Those who step across are those who are greater than John.

A New Power

The least will be citizens of the Kingdom of God. They will receive a new power with a new covenant. The new covenant with the empowerment of the Spirit is the sign of the fulfillment of the promises of God for the new era—the Kingdom era. In this new era, all those who follow Jesus will be the recipients of the Holy Spirit who will be poured out. They will be a new covenant Kingdom people who are clothed with power to become witnesses of the Gospel to all the world. In fact, the people of God receiving power from the infilling of the Holy Spirit is the primary characteristic of the new covenant Kingdom people (see Acts 2:14–39; Isaiah 59:19–21; Numbers 11:29; Jeremiah 31:33–34).

The book of Acts tells us about the historic moment and the impact that it had when the Holy Spirit came in fulfillment of Jesus' prophetic direction to His disciples:

> And while staying with them he ordered them not to depart from Jerusalem, but to wait for the promise of the Father, which, he said, "you heard from me; for John baptized with water, but you will be baptized with the Holy Spirit not many days from now. . . . But you will receive power when the Holy Spirit has come upon you, and you will be my witnesses in Jerusalem and in all Judea and Samaria, and to the end of the earth."
>
> Acts 1:4–8

Luke records the supernatural event that took place on the day of Pentecost:

> When the day of Pentecost arrived, they were all together in one place. And suddenly there came from heaven a sound like a mighty rushing wind, and it filled the entire house where they were sitting. And divided tongues as of fire appeared to them and rested on each one of them. And they were all filled with the Holy Spirit and began to speak in other tongues as the Spirit gave them utterance.
>
> Acts 2:1–4

Having been filled with the Holy Spirit, Peter stands and explains this supernatural event to the astonished and confused crowds at Jerusalem. He informs his audience about the wider meaning of Jesus' coming into the world—Jesus came and died to give us the new covenant in which we all receive the Holy Spirit being poured out with power.

This outpouring, Peter says, is "for you and for your children and for all who are far off, everyone whom the Lord our God calls to himself" (Acts 2:39). In other words, the gift of the Spirit is for all generations, regardless of gender, age, ethnicity or socioeconomic status. All who receive Jesus will receive the prophetic Spirit who will empower them to preach the Gospel, cast out demons, heal the sick and prophesy as Jesus did.

The prophet Joel prophesied this pouring out of the Spirit:

> "And it shall come to pass afterward, that I will pour out my Spirit on all flesh; your sons and your daughters shall prophesy, your old men shall dream dreams, and your young men shall see visions. Even on the male and female servants in those days I will pour out my Spirit."
>
> Joel 2:28–29

The Holy Spirit empowers the followers of Jesus to hear God's voice, to prophesy, to experience revelatory dreams and to see visions. The gift of the Spirit brings personal revelatory encounters with God. Joel also says the gift of the Spirit is the identifying mark of the people of God in those days. What are *those* days? The new era. The new covenant, Kingdom era!

The fulfillment of Joel's prophecy also fulfills Moses' prophetic prayer. "I wish that all the LORD's people were prophets and that the LORD would put his Spirit on them" (Numbers 11:29 NIV). Moses and the prophet Joel saw that the Kingdom era would be marked by the Spirit creating a prophetic community of supernaturally empowered people.

The prophet Isaiah declares that when the new covenant is established, the Holy Spirit, the Spirit of prophecy and power, will be upon God's people. God's powerful prophetic words will be in their mouths for all generations to come.

> "As for Me, this is My covenant with them," says the LORD: "My Spirit who is upon you, and My words which I have put in your mouth shall not depart from your mouth, nor from the mouth of your offspring, nor from the mouth of your offspring's offspring," says the LORD, "from now and forever."
>
> Isaiah 59:21 NASB

The pouring out of the Holy Spirit is a reinstatement of a people who hear God's voice. The new covenant of the Spirit is the answer to the question that was posed in the Garden that asked if we will hear and live by every word that proceeds from the mouth of God (see Genesis 3; Deuteronomy 8:3; Matthew 4:4). The answer is yes. When they receive the Holy Spirit, they will have the power to hear, obey and give witness to Jesus in a new era.

The Holy Spirit being poured out created a people of God who were now empowered to prophesy, heal the sick, cast out demons and perform miracles, signs and wonders in the name of Jesus. They received a new power and were mighty in word and deed, which follows the example of Jesus and His disciples.

Jesus is the Anointed One. During His life on earth, He was anointed with the Holy Spirit by whose power He cast out demons, healed the sick, worked miracles, spoke prophetic words and revelations and announced the Kingdom of God with signs and wonders. The least are those who follow Jesus, who step into the new era, who receive a new power and who are an ever-growing company of disciples in the expansion of the Church through prophetic witness, signs, wonders and miracles.[3]

A New Authority

In California there is a law regarding *adverse possession*. Adverse possession is another way of saying "squatters' rights." A squatter is someone who decides to take over a vacant or abandoned property without the owner's permission. If the owner does nothing about it or is slow in doing something about it (sometimes they do not even know it is happening), the squatter can take legal ownership. They can claim that they have upgraded the property by spending time on it. By setting up a home, however makeshift, they can claim to have improved the property by watching over it.

It is a legal nightmare for the actual owner of the property. The idea behind the laws regarding adverse possession that were written in 1979 by the California Courts of Appeals is that land use has been favored historically over land disuse. The person who uses or occupies the land is preferred in the law over the one who does not.

In biblical imagery, the sole of the foot is symbolic of dominion or authority over a person or place. The act of treading is an act of laying claim or taking possession. When the Bible speaks of things being under our feet it is using another image of authority and dominion. When an ancient king conquered another ruler, for example, he would place his foot on the neck of his defeated foe as a sign of his victory and dominion over him (see Joshua 10:24; 1 Kings 5:3).

The Bible uses this imagery when it prophesies of the day when our great enemy will be defeated finally and absolutely. When Messiah comes, all authority and dominion will be given to Him. All of His enemies will be underneath His feet (see Psalm 110:1; Hebrews 1:13; Malachi 4:3; Psalm 8:4–6). The New Testament uses the imagery to stress the authority of Jesus over all things.

What is authority? Simply put, authority is power. The New Testament uses the Greek word *exousia* 108 times, and the way that I explain the term is the right to rule and the freedom to act, the power of attorney by the name of Jesus, the power to issue a command and see that command obeyed, the legal right to take charge, and the permission granted by God to make decisions and judgments that are backed by supernatural, miracle-working power.

Having authority gives you the right and freedom to govern. In the life of Jesus, His authority allowed Him to turn water into wine, multiply bread, still storms, heal disease, cast out demons, resurrect the dead and defeat the enemy forever.

Authority originates from God. It is not a societal invention. It existed before the creation of the world because God is the ultimate power and authority. The universe—earth, angels, humans, animals, plants and the weather—was created by God's power and authority.

Then God created humans in His image and gave them authority. He gave them the authority to carry the image of God and to represent Him on the earth. He gave them authority to take dominion over all creation to steward the good that God had made. In the Garden, however, they lost that authority.

The enemy took humankind's authority by crafting a lie that sounded close enough to the truth that Adam and Eve believed it. He had been cast out of heaven and had come to earth with no authority of his own; however, he saw that humans carried the image of God and had been given God's authority on the earth. He could see that the future was not his, so he put his foot down in the Garden and took humankind's authority.

The minute we listen to and obey another voice, we forfeit our authority. The enemy stole the authority given us by God when Adam and Eve put their faith in his word.

From that moment, the world and everything in it was subject to his command. Satan stood on the earth in place of humanity and took dominion over what never belonged to him. He is a squatter!

He was mistaken, however, in thinking that the land was abandoned. The owner was about to take action by sending His Son. After receiving the Holy Spirit, Jesus began to put His foot down and exercise His authority on earth as it is in heaven. The process of taking back His authority had begun. How can we be sure? We see the witness of it when He casts out demons and heals the sick (see Matthew 8:16), and when He rebukes the wind and the sea and they become still (Mark 4:41).

Jesus is the Son of the living God to whom all authority rightfully belongs. Hebrews 2 declares, "'You have crowned him with glory and honor, putting *everything in subjection under his feet.' Now in putting everything in subjection to him, he left nothing outside of his control"* (verses 7–8, emphasis added). Revelation 12 concludes, "Now the salvation and the power and the kingdom of our God and the authority of his Christ have come, for the accuser of our brothers has been thrown down" (verse 10).

Paul tells us that Jesus was raised from the dead and is seated "far above all rule and authority and power and dominion, and above every name that is named, not only in this age but also in the one to come. *And he put all things under his feet"* (Ephesians 1:21–22, emphasis added).

All authority has been restored rightfully to Jesus; therefore, He says to those who are the least in this new Kingdom age, "I have given you authority to tread on serpents and scorpions, and over all the power of the enemy, and nothing shall hurt you" (Luke 10:19). He also says that He gives us power and authority to cast all demons out and to heal disease and affliction (see Matthew 10:1; Mark 6:7; Luke 9:1).

We are the ones who are called the least! We are living in the new age with new power and all authority given to us by Jesus. It is time for us to put our feet down fearlessly and evict the squatter who has taken up illegal residence on the earth.

Summary Points

1. Signs, wonders and miracles bear witness to the Kingdom of God having come.

2. The miracles of Jesus were a sign of a new era that was a dividing line.

3. When Jesus was born, Herod the Great, the most powerful man at the time, sought to assassinate Him. Herod understood that the birth of Christ was a divine political coup that would upend his rule and shift the power base.

4. John the Baptist was the prophet sent to prepare the way of the Lord—the prophesied Elijah to come. Yet John was the last of his kind and the sign of an end of an era.

5. No one was greater than John in his era, but in the new era, even the least is greater than John.

6. The least will be citizens of the Kingdom of God who receive a new power with a new covenant. They will be a new covenant Kingdom people who are clothed with power to become witnesses of the Gospel to all the world.

7. Jesus came and died to give us the new covenant in which we all receive the outpouring of the Holy Spirit with power. All who receive Jesus will receive the prophetic Spirit who will empower them to preach the Gospel, cast out demons, heal the sick and prophesy as Jesus did.

8. The gift of the Spirit is the identifying mark of the people of God in the new Kingdom era.

9. In the new era of the Kingdom, all authority has been restored rightfully to Jesus. He says to those who are the least in this new Kingdom age that He has given us

authority to cast out demons and to heal disease and affliction. *We are the least* living in the new age with new power and all authority given to us by Jesus.

Questions and Activation

1. Set some time aside for reflection. Have a journal and a Bible available. Record your answers, thoughts and anything the Lord says to you during this time.

2. Invite the Holy Spirit into your reflection time. Think and reflect on what it means to be "the least" in the Kingdom of God. Think and reflect on your own life in relation to miracles, signs and wonders that bear witness to Jesus and the people of the Kingdom.

3. Answer the questions below.

   * Have you been clothed with the new power and authority of the Kingdom?
   * When was the last time you prayed for the sick and they were healed?
   * Have you received the infilling of or baptism in the Holy Spirit?
   * Are you willing and ready to be empowered by the Holy Spirit and to participate in the mission of Jesus?
   * Are there any doctrinal beliefs or personal fears that have prevented you in any way from receiving the infilling of the Holy Spirit?

Read and Meditate

Joel 2:28–29; John 14:26; Luke 24:45–49; Acts 1–2; 8:14–17; 10:34–46; 19:1–7

Activation

"Ask, and it will be given you. . . . Everyone who asks receives" (Luke 11:9–10). Believe that God will fill you with the Spirit the moment that you ask. Expect to receive the gifts of the Holy Spirit with the infilling: prophecy, tongues, healing, etc.

Jesus said, "If you then, who are evil, know how to give good gifts to your children, how much more will the heavenly Father give the Holy Spirit to those who ask him!" (Luke 11:13). Being filled with the Holy Spirit is not a strange, difficult or extraordinary thing for a believer.

On the day of Pentecost, the Holy Spirit was poured out (meaning sent or given in fullness) to those who followed Jesus. This was to empower them for life and service in the Kingdom of God.

Scripture tells of many baptisms, many infillings of the Spirit. We receive the Spirit from God who supplies (and continues to supply) us with the Spirit to sustain us to the end (see Galatians 3:2–5). So whether or not you have ever received the infilling of the Spirit, you can receive a fresh infilling right now.

Jesus is asking you to take a step of faith and receive the Holy Spirit.

- Before praying for the infilling, spend some time coming into agreement with what Scripture emphasizes about the Holy Spirit and His gifts.
- Posture your heart in faith to receive with expectation.

- As you pray, know that the Lord hears your prayer. He is ready to fill you with the Spirit.
- Be spiritually sensitive to the presence of the Spirit who will come upon you.
- You might want to take a few moments to worship the Lord quietly and respond to His presence.
- Finally, invite the Holy Spirit to fill and empower you afresh.

Pray

Father, in the name of Jesus, I come now to be filled with the Holy Spirit. There is nothing in my life I want more. You have promised that everyone who asks will receive, so here I am. I am asking; therefore, I expect to receive. When I begin to speak, I will act in faith and pray in tongues as Your Spirit gives me utterance. I will not be afraid. Right now, in the name of Jesus, I receive the Holy Spirit. I believe that I have received.

- When you have prayed, allow the Spirit to speak and pray through you in tongues and prophecy. Act in bold faith and begin to speak. Yield to the Spirit flowing in and through your being and allow a natural flow of supernatural words. Do not to be fearful, but cooperate fully with the Spirit by speaking out confidently in faith.
- Spend some time thanking God for filling you.
- Expect that you have received.
- Listen for the voice of God, and obey what He tells you.

CHAPTER 5

Conflict Is Unavoidable

"For nation will rise against nation, and kingdom against
kingdom, and there will be famines and earthquakes in
various places."

Matthew 24:7

"From the days of John the Baptist until now the kingdom of
heaven has suffered violence."

Matthew 11:12

I t was quite unexpected. In fact, it was so unexpected that
it caused me to question whether I had heard correctly.
I was experiencing an anointed time of worship when it
happened. I had asked the Lord what He wanted to do.
I want to increase the anointing on the worship leader.
As soon as my hand alighted on her shoulder, the tiny young
woman with the face of an angel who had moments before
been leading the crowd in powerful worship began to manifest
demonically. Dropping onto her hands and knees, her face and

body contorted into something akin to a gargoyle. Her hands became claws, and her voice became deep, thick and demonic. She growled, snarled and roared. On all fours, she postured in front of me for maximum intimidation. I do not like demons. I do not like their violence and bullying.

"You will be still and silent *now* in Jesus' name!" I whispered this ferociously in her ear. Immediately she froze, and the growling ceased. I called her by her name to engage her apart from the demon, and then led her in prayer. The Lord spoke to me that she had been in agreement with a number of lies, and I walked her through the process of stepping out of agreement with those lies. With tears and a few shudders, she was released from years of demonic oppression, depression and self-hatred. In her youth, she had been the victim of sexual violence that she had hidden for many years. On top of that, her pain had been compounded by religion, unforgiveness, self-hatred and promiscuity. The enemy had sought to destroy her and the call upon her life by violence—but God had a different plan.

The enemy seeks to destroy all of us. He tries to mar our lives through sin, sickness or evil, through war, child abuse, cancer, murder, racism, addiction, sex trafficking, terrorism, genocide, abortion, persecution—the list of atrocities inflicted on humanity by purveyors of evil seems endless. These are only a few examples of the works of darkness. But Jesus came to destroy the works of darkness (see 1 John 3:8).

Since the Beginning

Every move of God is met with resistance from the enemy. There is no such thing as faith without opposition. There is no such thing as a revival without resistance. Revival always disrupts the status quo, and it uncovers the works of darkness in the lives of individuals, people groups, governments and nations. This happens because the Kingdom of God is a dividing line. No one can stand with a foot in the world and a foot in the Kingdom at the same time. The King of the Kingdom seeks to rob the darkness of its prisoners, while the devil seeks to stop Him and increase the darkness.

Jesus told us that the least in the Kingdom is greater than John. This means that the supernatural power and divine authority the citizens of the Kingdom receive is greater than John had. At the same time, He warned us that the Kingdom of God suffers violence. As R. T. France explains, "While John was the last of the old order, his fate was the foretaste of the conflicts which are already beginning to affect the new order."[1]

This should not be a surprise. Violence is certainly nothing new. We are in a war. Conflict is unavoidable. When the Kingdom comes, it ushers in a new government, a new order and new-covenant people who are ruled by a new King.

Jesus understands. He is saying that living a life of righteousness in a world that is dominated by evil and darkness means living contrary to political correctness and cultural convention. It will result in persecution.[2] Paul says, "Indeed, all who desire to live a godly life in Christ Jesus will be persecuted, while evil people and impostors will go on from bad to worse, deceiving and being deceived" (2 Timothy 3:12–13). When Jesus told us that the Kingdom of God suffers violence, He was acknowledging a pattern of action and response. This pattern is found throughout Scripture. God begins to move, and the enemy resists and opposes what He is doing. It has been this way since the beginning.

In the Garden, man was made in the image of God, was blessed by God and then was given dominion over all that God had created. Idyllic. Serene. Peaceful. Enter the serpent and a political coup. A coup is a sudden and often violent illegal political action that results in a change of government by force. The illegal actions taken by the serpent gained him rulership over creation. God rendered judgment. Moses records the sentencing of the serpent, "I will put enmity between you and the woman, and between your offspring and her offspring; he shall bruise your head, and you shall bruise his heel" (Genesis 3:15).

The verdict? There will be perpetual hostility and violence until the Kingdom of God is realized fully. The heavens and the earth, along with all of humanity, are involved in a cosmic war. In the end, the seed of the woman—Jesus Christ—and all those in Christ will have the victory. Until then, the Kingdom of God suffers violence.

Cosmic Conflict

At this point, it is important to have a discussion about cosmic conflict, which is the war that encompasses the cosmos and involves both those who are seen and those who are unseen. Let's be clear. There is only one Creator, God the Father. The Old Testament, however, is full of references to other gods or deities, as well as a heavenly council and army (see 2 Chronicles 2:5; Psalm 95:3; 1 Chronicles 16:25). Some scholars contend that many of these deities were set over nations originally to rule on behalf of God the Father. At some point they rebelled against God and were, therefore, no longer considered to be legitimate sons of God. They have instead become known as demons.[3]

In the book of Daniel, we discover through an angelic messenger that Daniel's prayers were resisted for three weeks by "the prince of the kingdom of Persia" (Daniel 10:13). This prince was not an earthly prince. Evidently, there was a spiritual prince (think powerful demon) set against the plans of God and the prayers of God's servant. There is conflict in the unseen realms over the God's agenda on the earth. As Gregory Boyd points out,

While modern Western believers tend to separate the "spiritual realm" from the "the natural realm," [Ancient Near East] people, including ancient Jews, had a more holistic perspective. Throughout the Bible "earthly" and "heavenly" battles were viewed as two dimensions of one and the same battle. . . . As [Walter] Wink correctly notes, the prevailing assumption in the biblical narrative is that "what occurs on earth has its corollary in the heavens."[4]

This understanding is reflected in the Old Testament. We also find this understanding about a cosmic conflict on earth as it is in heaven in the words of Jesus and the New Testament writers. They testify to rulers, authorities, powers and principalities, not to mention Satan himself (the god of this age). Satan and these demons with various levels of power and authority have a clear agenda, and that is to influence and rule all earthly kingdoms, as well as to lie, steal, kill and destroy God's plans and people.

Paul counsels us that Satan is not only the god of this world who blinds the minds of the unbeliever, but he is also the ruler of the power of the air who works in the sons of disobedience (see Ephesians 6:12; 1 John 5:19; 2 Corinthians 4:4; Ephesians 2:2). Satan and his demonic subjects work to bring all the nations and all of humanity into bondage to darkness, deception, sin and evil (see Revelation 13:3–14). In light of this truth, Paul instructs us not to be ignorant of the enemy's devices and schemes against us (see 2 Corinthians 2:11). We are to be aware of and remember that Satan prowls around like a roaring lion seeking whom he may devour (see 1 Peter 5:8). Therefore, we are to put on the full armor of God (see Ephesians 6:11–13), use the weapons of our warfare that are mighty for pulling down strongholds (see 2 Corinthians 10:4), and fight the good fight of faith (see 1 Timothy 6:12).

Again, Boyd sums it up succinctly:

Everything about Jesus and the early church presupposed a cosmic-conflict worldview in which God had to battle powers to establish his will "on earth as it is in heaven" and that God's people have a significant role to play in bringing this about.[5]

Conflict is, indeed, unavoidable.

Spiritual Warfare

Jesus knew conflict was unavoidable. He came to conquer the powers of darkness and depose their ruler. In fact, His entire ministry was an act of war against the elements of darkness. He was the light that came into the darkness, and the darkness could not overcome Him (see John 1:4–5). His preaching of the Gospel and demonstrations of power all signaled the overthrow of Satan's rule and dominion.

The Kingdom of God as an agent of spiritual warfare is a major theme in Jesus' life. He actively and intentionally went about displacing the works of the devil in both His teaching and His ministry. The Kingdom of God and the kingdom of Satan coexist on earth. They are both powerful, but they are not equal. One is defeated. One is victorious. The Kingdom of God is overcoming the kingdom of Satan even as we speak. When Jesus healed the blind man, cast out the legion of demons and raised Lazarus from the dead, He was establishing the new rule, the new order. This is what He meant when He said that the Kingdom of God has come upon us (see Luke 11:20).

The Pharisees accused Jesus of operating by the power of Beelzebub (Satan) after He cast out a demon that had caused a man to be blind and mute. He gave the religious rulers the following explanation:

"But if it is by the Spirit of God that I cast out demons, then the kingdom of God has come upon you. Or how can someone

enter a strong man's house and plunder his goods, unless he first binds the strong man? Then indeed he may plunder his house."

Matthew 12:28–29, emphasis added

Jesus bound the strongman and plundered the kingdom of darkness with every powerful word and deed. As Clinton E. Arnold explains, "The redemptive reign of God was beginning in the person and mission of the Lord Jesus."[6]

Jesus was not only establishing the rule of God, but He was leading a prison break for those who had been held in darkness behind bars of demonic rule. Micah, the prophet, prophesied that there would be one who would breach the gate to make a way for the King to lead His sheep out (see Micah 2:13).

John the Baptist had been sent ahead of Jesus to prepare the way. He was the bridge maker who called people to repentance. Repentance broke open the hearts of the people, which in turn opened the possibility for them to receive the Kingdom of God and its King.

We know Jesus said, "the kingdom of God suffers violence." Violence in this passage is the word *biazo*.[7] This word carries a sense of breaking forth.

The Kingdom was breaking in through Jesus by the power of the Spirit. Those who received Him and His Kingdom were led in a violent breaking out from under the rule of Satan. The violent suffering (or breaking forth) in Matthew is related to the violent breaking forth in Micah.

The picture formed by the prophecy in Micah is of a shepherd leading the sheep through a breach in a wall. The sheep are so eager to get out that they crowd, push and kick their way through. They *break forth*. It is a violent escape. It is a prison break. Those who have escaped violently then turn and help others do likewise. The escapees become the "violent" Jesus identifies in the second half of Matthew 11:12.

The prison warden was not pleased. He arranged for a violent confrontation of his own. Though not equal in power or authority, the enemy resisted and opposed Jesus continuing the pattern that is identified throughout this chapter and that is acknowledged by Jesus in Matthew's gospel. As Jesus went about doing good, the enemy stirred up antagonism, hostility and violence against Him. Jesus was arrested, beaten, mocked and crucified. In a diabolical twist, the King was dead. His followers were confused. All seemed lost. Satan was victorious.

It Is Not Over Yet

Three days later, the resurrection of Jesus changed everything. The cross was not the *coup de grace* of the kingdom of darkness but rather of the Kingdom of God. Jesus suffered violence unto death voluntarily to conquer the grave on our behalf. In doing so, He became the victor of the cosmic contest that sealed the fate of Satan and ensured the final consummation of the Kingdom of God. Hallelujah!

It is imperative to understand, however, that the conflict with darkness did not begin on the cross and does not end with the resurrection. The author of Hebrews explains that everything is *being* put in subjection to Him. Nothing will be left outside of His control, even though at present we do not see that everything is in subjection to Him (see Hebrews 2:8). Why? The inaugurated Kingdom is already but not yet realized fully. This means that the Kingdom of God still suffers violence and will continue to do so until Jesus returns once more.

After the resurrection and before His ascension, Jesus announces to His disciples that He has been given all authority in the cosmos and is sending them out into the world to make more disciples (see Matthew 28:18–20). He assures them that He and His authority will be with them as they go. He gave His disciples a similar message when He gave them authority to heal every disease and affliction and to cast out every demon (see Matthew 10:1–8). We are to understand that while the battle belongs to the Lord, it will now be fought by His followers. We continue His mission.

Moves of God will be enacted by followers of Christ. These moves will advance the Kingdom of God and will overthrow the works of darkness as the enemy resists and opposes. Yes, victory is assured. But conflict is unavoidable.

Some in the Church today have not understood the inevitability and the necessity of the Body of Christ's involvement and engagement in spiritual warfare. Some ignore or deny the reality of spiritual beings set violently against the will of God for our lives individually and corporately. It can be uncomfortable. It can also be a snare as some seem to find a demon under every rock.

Even so, ignorance is not bliss. In this case, it might be deadly. Whether or not we choose to deny or ignore this reality, the battle affects us, our families, our communities and the nations of the earth. Evil is alive and well. Following Jesus is not a game—it is a war. Lives are at stake.

When Jesus declared, "From the days of John the Baptist until now the kingdom of heaven has suffered violence," He added, "and the violent take it by force" (Matthew 11:12). Not only does He allude to a pattern of action and reaction, but He also brings revelation to our table. He reveals the timing that has been seen from the inauguration of the Kingdom until its consummation. He reveals the nature of the conflict, which is the violent opposition to the overthrow of darkness and its ruler on the earth. Finally, He reveals the identity of those who engage. They are an empowered people as ferocious and bold as their opponent. In the next chapter, we will discuss engagement and what becoming "the violent" means for the Body of Christ. You may be surprised. First, however, we must take a look within.

The War Within

For over a year, I kept hearing the Lord say, *Revival looks like the story of Gideon in the book of Judges.*

I thought, *What does Gideon have to do with revival?* I asked Him to help me understand.

In the story of Gideon, we find the people of God under the hand of an oppressive enemy (see Judges 6). For seven years, their crops had been devoured, their livestock had been stolen and their land had been laid waste. They were under political oppression and in a national decline. They were in an economic depression, and they were hungry, suffering and afraid. They cried out to God for help.

God sends a prophet, which is not what we would expect. It seems out of place. Prophets, however, play the significant role of calling people back into covenant relationship with God. They foretell what is coming in the future, and they forthtell present realities according to God's perspective.

The prophecy in Gideon's narrative has two parts. First, God told the people to remember who He was and what He has done. He led them out from the house of slavery in Egypt. He delivered them from the hand of the Egyptians and all who oppressed them. God used the prophet to point out that while they were presently under the hand of an oppressor, He had delivered them from a situation like this before. God asked His people whose hand was mightier, His or the hand of their oppressor? They had forgotten that their God was mighty to deliver.

The second part of the prophecy is an indictment. God says the people had not obeyed. Moses instructed them about the blessings they would receive if they obey the commandments of the Lord, and conversely, about the curses they would receive if they did not. Joshua, after entering into the Promised Land, challenged them to choose to obey the Lord as they lived among pagans. Yet we find that the people did what was evil in the sight of the Lord. They abandoned God and bowed down to the idols of the land. There is a name for this. It is called apostasy.

The Greater Threat

Apostasy is greater than any threat from any enemy on the outside, because it is a sign of being defeated on the inside. Apostasy is the renouncing or abandoning of faith, and it breeds ever-increasing evil. When we live by our own rules and only for ourselves, evil runs rampant, morality erodes and lawlessness abounds in our cities, nations and families.

The sign of impending apostasy is idolatry, which is when we give our worship, attention, affection or resources to something other than God in order to gain personal power, riches, gratification or sexual favor. It is dependence on anything other than God for our needs, wants and advancement.

In this passage, God heard the cry of His people and responded by revealing to them that it was the enemy within that made them vulnerable to the enemy without. Israel was in danger of collapsing as a nation not because of the Midianites, but because they had compromised with the culture and had turned away from God. Their economy had been devastated, and in their distress, they had turned to an idol for help. Somewhere along the way, they chose to deal with fear and insecurity in this manner.

Throughout history, people have compromised politically, morally, socially and spiritually with culture due to fear and the uncertainty of their times. They do not recognize the evil that is rising in their midst. "Gradually, though no one remembers exactly how it happened, the unthinkable becomes tolerable. And then acceptable. And then legal. And then applaudable."[8]

Compromise and accommodation of the culture overthrows wholehearted devotion to Jesus and His Gospel truth, which disempowers the believer. This process renders believers powerless to destroy the work of the devil. The sin within is the greatest threat to the life of God's people. It removes our influence, authority, prophetic voice and our ability to be the salt and the light in darkness.

It is time we get it back. Revival looks like a return to whole-hearted devotion to Jesus with a fresh empowerment from the Holy Spirit. We need to return to what Jesus did, which was demonstrating the Gospel and overthrowing darkness.

Summary Points

1. Every move of God is met with resistance from the enemy. There is no such thing as faith without opposition or revival without resistance. Revival disrupts the status quo and uncovers the works of darkness in the lives of individuals, people groups, governments and nations.

2. We are in a war. Conflict is unavoidable. When the Kingdom comes, it ushers in a new government, a new order and new-covenant people who are ruled by a new King and who are opposed by the devil.

3. Jesus tells us that the Kingdom of God suffers violence, revealing a pattern of action and response that is found throughout Scripture. God begins to move, and the enemy resists and opposes what God is doing. It has been this way since the beginning.

4. There will be perpetual hostility and violence until the Kingdom of God is fully consummate. The heavens, the earth and all of humanity are involved in a cosmic war, involving both what is seen and what is unseen.

5. Satan and demons, who have various levels of power and authority, have a clear agenda—to influence and rule all earthly kingdoms and to lie, steal, kill and destroy God's plans and people. Satan is not only the god of this world who blinds the minds of the unbeliever, but he is also the ruler of the power of the air. He works in the sons of disobedience to bring all of the nations and all of humanity into bondage to darkness, deception, sin and evil.

6. A major theme in the life of Jesus is that the Kingdom of God is to be an agent of spiritual warfare. He went about displacing the works of the devil actively and

intentionally. When Jesus healed the blind man, cast out the legion of demons and raised Lazarus from the dead, He was establishing the new rule, the new order, which was the Kingdom of God.

7. Jesus suffered violence unto death voluntarily to conquer the grave on our behalf. In doing so, He became the victor of the cosmic contest and sealed the fate of Satan. He ensured the final consummation of the Kingdom of God. The conflict with darkness did not begin on the cross and does not end with the resurrection. The inaugurated Kingdom is already but not yet realized fully. This means that the Kingdom of God still suffers violence and will continue to do so until Jesus returns once more.

8. After the resurrection but before His ascension, Jesus announces to His disciples that He has been given all authority in the cosmos and is sending them out into the world to make more disciples (see Matthew 28:18–20). We are intended to understand that the battle belongs to the Lord, but it will now be fought by His followers as we continue His mission.

Questions and Activation

1. Set some time aside for reflection. Have a journal and a Bible available. Record your answers, thoughts and anything the Lord says to you during this time.

2. Invite the Holy Spirit into your reflection time. Think and reflect on the last section of this chapter, "The Greater Threat." Think and reflect on the statement, "The truth is, the sin within is the greatest threat to the life of God's people. It removes our influence, authority,

prophetic voice and ability to be the salt and the light
in darkness."

3. Think and reflect on more of Gideon's story.

In Judges 6:11–13, we discover that Gideon is part
of a new generation that has a disempowered legacy.
Judges 2:10 gives us a clue when it says, "That generation also were gathered to their fathers. And there
arose another generation after them who did not know
the LORD or the work that he had done for Israel."

An angel came to Gideon with a message saying,
"The LORD is with you, O mighty man of valor" (Judges
6:12). Rather than being amazed or fearful, Gideon
does not seem to understand the divine nature of the
visitation. His response is incredulous and sarcastic.
"Where are all his wonderful deeds that our fathers
recounted to us, saying, 'Did not the LORD bring us up
from Egypt?' But now the LORD has forsaken us and
given us into the hand of Midian" (verse 13).

He is essentially saying, "Yeah, right. I suppose you
are going to try to tell me all those old stories are true."
The angel proclaimed that God exists and that He is
going to go with Gideon in supernatural signs, wonders
and miracles. Gideon's response to this good news,
however, was that God is either nonexistent or absent.

Why was Gideon jaded? Gideon was part of a generation that had been experiencing severe political,
cultural and economic oppression. They had not experienced the great Exodus. His father and his father's
generation had handed down the testimonies, but ap-
parently Gideon did not believe them.

A testimony is the retelling of an actual experience
as a witness of the power of God. The testimony of
Jesus and His saving power in our lives is the spirit of

prophecy. The testimony prophesies that if God did it for one of us, He will do it for another. He is no respecter of persons (see Acts 10:34), and He is the same yesterday, today and forever (see Hebrews 13:8). There is power in testimony.

For Gideon, the testimony had no power. He had no confidence in his father's God, because he had no confidence in his father's testimony. His father, the elders, the leaders and the community were apostate. They were worshiping idols and not the God of wonders. Their practice contradicted their testimony. They were not living in the worship and power of their God. They could not say that if God did it for us, He will do it for you. In fact, the reason for the political, cultural and economic oppression was the apostasy and idolatry of the nation.

4. Answer the questions below.

   - In what ways have I abandoned faith in God?
   - In what ways have I compromised with culture?
   - Have I left my first love?
   - Have I grown lukewarm?
   - Has the violence, intimidation, cultural pressure to conform, vitriolic accusations, constant bullying and human reasoning of my day numbed me to what is right and holy before God?
   - Am I living as salt and light to those around me?
   - Have I become cynical and distrustful of those who are called fathers, elders, leaders and those in authority?
   - Am I am bowing down to the idols of my day?

Read and Meditate

Matthew 24:12; Revelation 2:3–5; 3

Activation

Jesus, Paul, James and John tell us that our lives are letters written to the world and that they bear witness to what we believe and worship. In other words, our lives speak a language more powerful than words. It is the loudest sermon you will ever preach.

> Therefore, since we are surrounded by so great a cloud of witnesses, let us also lay aside every weight, and sin which clings so closely, and let us run with endurance the race that is set before us, looking to Jesus, the founder and perfecter of our faith, who for the joy that was set before him endured the cross, despising the shame, and is seated at the right hand of the throne of God.
>
> Hebrews 12: 1–2

Pray

1. Invite the Holy Spirit to search your heart and mind to "see if there be any grievous way" in you (Psalm 139:24).

2. Ask God to give you godly sorrow that leads to repentance and produces fear of God, longing and zeal (see 2 Corinthians 7:10–11).

3. Repent for all sin related to apostasy and idolatry that was revealed through your answer to the questions

above. Ask the Lord to forgive, cleanse and renew you for

- abandoning your faith and becoming compromised by the flesh or the culture.
- giving your attention and resources to entertainment, sports, work, fame, fortune, promotion, sexual sin, etc.
- living a life that disempowers your testimony.
- not being salt and light in your sphere of influence with family, friends or co-workers.
- being lukewarm in your faith.
- leaving your first love.
- anything else the Holy Spirit shows you.

4. Declare:
   - I will no longer conform to this world, but I will be transformed *now* by the renewing of my mind (see Romans 12:2).
   - I will not be conformed to my former ways, but I will be obedient and holy as He is holy (see 1 Peter 1:14–15).
5. Thank God for His forgiveness.[9]
6. Invite the Holy Spirit to cleanse and renew your mind.
7. Spend some time in worship allowing the presence of the Lord to comfort you.

CHAPTER 6

Kingdom Violence

"And the violent take it by force."

Matthew 11:12

REVOLUTION: a violent overthrow of a government or social order in favor of a new system; a sudden or momentous change in any situation.

There is power in the name of Jesus! He is the same yesterday, today and forever!" I shouted these words in the little sanctuary as the Spirit lifted my heart toward healing. The evening before, hundreds of people had attended a very large meeting that my team and I hosted. Many in attendance were healed. This night, however, the team and I arrived to find a small gathering in a modest building in a destitute neighborhood.

As I was delivering the message, I could feel the presence of the Lord in the room. A knowing in my heart burst upon my mind. It was time to follow the Spirit.

"The Lord is here to heal *right now*," I announced. I then released a prayer inviting the Spirit to heal every sickness and disease in the room. "Stand up and try to do what you could not do before. See if you have been healed."

One man in the back stood declaring that his eye pain was gone. Others began to shout out testimonies of healing. The ministry team went throughout the room laying hands on people and continued to pray for healing, and there were shouts and tears and rejoicing.

All of a sudden, a man stood and began walking awkwardly and haltingly around the room pushing a walker. His body and feet were twisted. His legs seemed to get tangled up in each other every few steps. Several people tried to stop him, but he pushed through them determined to continue his furious journey.

Another man ran to the platform asking to speak.

"I have known this man for years," he began. "In all the years I have known him, he has never even stood up. He has a childhood brain injury."

The man with the twisted body allowed no one to help or stop him as he continued to make his way around the sanctuary. Jesus was healing him. It was a miracle!

Miracles are part of the Kingdom, and like the Kingdom, they are not limited to ministry venues. Far from it.

I had another miraculous encounter a few years back with a driver who had been tasked to take me to the airport. She was waiting for me as I stepped out of my hotel eager to get on the plane back to California and my family. As I got settled into the back seat, she started our drive to the airport.

"Hello there! What is your name?" I asked.

"Naomi," she replied.

"Naomi is a great biblical name," I commented.

"Yes, it is. I was named after Naomi in the Bible." She seemed engaged, and I felt the stirring of the Holy Spirit, so I decided to throw out a hook and go fishing.

"I am a minister, and I just finished writing a sermon on Naomi. Would you like to know what I discovered about your namesake? I think the Lord has a message for you in it because I am sensing from Him that you have had a life much like hers."

She took the bait. I could tell she was eager to know what the Lord might reveal to her. I told her what the Lord had showed me about Naomi in the Bible, and I explained how it might apply to her life. Naomi had experienced extreme hardship, poverty and loss, and she had taken the courageous risk of starting over. I then prophesied about a ministry call of God on her life. She began crying so hard that she missed the off-ramp to the airport. Once we made it to arrivals, I asked if I could pray for her. She said yes, but she also asked if she could tell me her story.

She was a strong woman who had created a great career for herself. But through several difficult circumstances, she had become unemployed and homeless. Being a driver was her last hope to rebuild. The night before our ride to the airport, she had heard the Lord whisper to her. He had said that He would speak clearly to her the following day. He did. He spoke through a perfect stranger. She testified that she knew now that everything was about to change. She had faith to believe, and she would fulfill the call on her life. The Kingdom of God had come near.

Miracle testimonies open our eyes to the power of God and His Kingdom. They give us courage and boldness. Sometimes, however, things do not happen the way we hoped that they would. I have seen God do miracles all over the world. I have laid hands on many who are sick, dying or demonized, and I have watched the Holy Spirit heal and set them free.

Therefore, when my mom was diagnosed with incurable cancer, I prayed with considerable faith. Over and over again I prayed. She did not get healed. For five long and agonizing years, she fought this enemy. Our family spent many sleepless nights at her side in the hospital. She went through disfiguring surgeries, endless chemotherapy sessions and frantic emergency room visits. Over time, she lost weight, hair, mobility and all quality of life. She never, however, lost faith. We kept praying for a miracle.

"Mrs. Mulloy, it is time to stop chemo and start hospice," the doctor said. "The treatments are hurting you more than they are helping you. We are afraid we may kill you if we do any more. I'm sorry." I watched it register on my family's faces. Confusion turned to fear.

"Then I'll just die," my mom said. Her words were equal parts question, factual statement and cry for help. In answer, the doctor assured her they would keep her comfortable. My dad tried to convince the doctor that she could tolerate more treatments, but the doctor held his ground kindly and necessarily. The three of us drove home in silence. We kept praying for a miracle, though. Mom received her miracle when she went to be with the Lord, which ended her intense and excruciating suffering. Yes, the Kingdom of God suffers violence.

Where We Are

We have come a long way in our discussion of the way of the kingdom. We have established that violence is a sign to us. It signals demonic opposition to God's agenda and His movement on the earth in and through His people. We have clarified that we are in a war in the midst of a cosmic conflict. In the last chapter, we talked about spiritual warfare, which led us to conclude that conflict was unavoidable for both Jesus and us.

Peter reminds us that it is not strange or alien for us as believers to experience fiery trials (see 1 Peter 4:12). We are to expect them. Even still, as Peter points out, they test us. They surprise us. They sometimes catch us off guard. Remember, even the formidable John the Baptist questioned if Jesus was the Messiah when he was facing violence.

How shall we respond to such things? Without fear. We are the least who are greater than John. We have been given a new covenant in which we receive the Holy Spirit, power and authority to face our enemy.

What are we to do? We become violent. When Jesus stated the Kingdom of God suffers violence, He finished the statement with "and the violent take it by force" (Matthew 11:12). Jon Ruthven clarifies this violence as expressing the connection between the Kingdom and those who would enter it. "They do so by aggressive, persistent faith . . . being led by the Spirit into a ministry of life and power in intimacy with God in Christ Jesus."[1] Just as Satan has a violent campaign to overthrow God and His works, there is an empowered and fearless people of God who will counter the opposition as violently.

Following Jesus is serious and sobering business. In the last chapter, you were given an opportunity to deal with any sin inside your heart that would cause vulnerability to the enemy from the outside. This was preparation to receive a fresh activation to help you step into the role that Jesus modeled for you. Being entangled in sin or compromising with culture muddies the heart and mind, and it blocks hearing and vision. Wisdom dictates that a clean heart is essential for engagement. It keeps motivations clean, ears open, vision clear and enemy access limited.

What does it mean to become those who do Kingdom violence? What are the implications for the Body of Christ? These questions and more are about to be addressed. The first order of business is to determine the difference between the violence that is done by the enemy and the Kingdom violence that is done by the least.

Dark Violence

Dark violence is the work of darkness. It is the devil and his cohorts deceiving, enticing, seducing, murdering, stealing and destroying. To help illustrate what this violence looks like, here are a few current real-life examples:

- 862,000 induced abortions were performed in the U.S. in 2017.[2] There have been more than 61.5 million babies aborted in the U.S. since 1973.[3] In many places, it is now becoming acceptable at any point in pregnancy. Some are born alive and left to die.[4] Their body parts are being sold for a profit.[5]
- Suicide is increasing. A 33 percent increase was recorded in death by suicide in the last two decades.[6]
- Pornography is epidemic. It is estimated that there are more than 2.5 million pornographic websites available today.[7] In 2016, 4.6 billion hours of pornography was viewed on one site alone.[8]
- Child sexual exploitation (known as "child porn") is one of the fastest-growing online businesses.[9]
- One million children globally are sold into sex slavery or forced labor every year, including over 20,000 in America. This amounts to more than 50 children per day.[10] An astonishing 50–60 percent come from America's foster care system.[11]
- The breakdown of marriage and family continues as 42–45 percent of marriages end in divorce.[12]
- Atheism, witchcraft and occultism are on the rise and in proportion to millennials who are rejecting Christianity.[13]
- Religious persecution, ethnic cleansing and holocaust still occurs. Terrorists kill Christians, Jews, Muslims,

Egyptians, Americans, French, British and others in the name of God, believing it is God's will and pleasure.

- Bride burning takes the life of one woman every hour in India, which results in more than 8,000 women killed per year.[14] And child brides as young as nine are forced to marry adult men in Africa. Child marriage affects 42 percent of girls.[15]
- Racism.
- Gender choice and confusion.
- A political spirit fostering bitter division and virulent hatred.
- The heroin epidemic in the high school in my neighborhood.
- A five-year-old little boy in North Carolina shot in the head execution style in broad daylight in front of his sisters by the neighbor because he rode his bike onto the neighbor's property.[16]
- My mom dying from cancer.
- A friend's family torn apart by their child who is terrorized by mental illness.
- A friend's addiction to alcohol and drugs that is destroying her marriage and family.

Consider also what I have observed in the Church. Worship leaders getting drunk backstage of a worship performance. Pastors using the foulest language or spiritually abusing their flock to gain favor, riches and fame. Sexual abuse perpetrated by narcissistic and predatory spiritual leaders who are often excused or ignored by those in authority. These are only a few examples of the works of darkness that are being perpetrated against people in the Church. Wherever you find disease, poverty, bondage, abuse and evil the enemy is at work.

The Revolution

Kingdom violence is different from the dark violence in the world. Jesus countered and overturned the works of darkness with every good work and miracle He performed. The way He lived His life was a revolution. Jesus lived and acted in a continuous insurgency against demonic rulers, authorities, principalities and powers and their violent effects on people. Even His death was an act of revolution and spiritual warfare. The cross was a deathblow to darkness. It guaranteed the imminent dethroning of all demonic dominion that opposed God's will on earth as it is in heaven (see Colossians 2:15).

The revolution was a lifestyle that includes entering deliberately and intentionally into the conflict with our real enemy. Gregory Boyd clarifies for us:

> On a physical level, it looked as if Jesus's conflict was with earthly authorities, but his *real* struggle—and . . . *our* real struggle—was against fallen powers that continually resist God's purpose and exercise a destructive influence in society and creation.[17]

It is imperative for us to understand this idea, right here and right now. If we do not, we might be found resisting God. Paul is emphatic when he tells us that our battle is not against flesh and blood people. Losing sight of the real enemy is how many have fallen into cooperation with "the cosmic powers over this present darkness, against the spiritual forces of evil in the heavenly places" (Ephesians 6:12). Opposing the plan of God is aligning with the plan of Satan.

Remember that John the Baptist and the culture of his day had very specific, even biblical, expectations for a revolution that would be led by the Messiah. They expected a militant rebellion against earthly enemies. They were looking for a king who would lead them to conquer all of Israel's sociopolitical oppressors and corrupt religious leaders. Peter must have had this in mind when he tried to dissuade Jesus from going to the cross saying, "Far be it from you, Lord!" (Matthew 16:22). In response, Peter receives the most shocking rebuke found in the book of Matthew. Jesus says, "Get behind me, Satan!" (Matthew 16:23).

Peter's focus and attention were on earthly things. He did not understand what the real threat to the Kingdom was, and he did not understand the real agenda of the Lord. Like the rest of Israel, he was expecting a revolution that would conquer flesh and blood. Flesh and blood, however, are the casualties of war, not who the enemy is. Jesus was going to the cross to conquer all demonic authorities to attain once and for all complete salvation for humanity. Jesus was moving toward total victory in the cosmic conflict. He was doing it with every powerful word He uttered and every deed He enacted. His life demonstrated Kingdom violence.

Kingdom Violence

In another encounter, Peter's example offers us clear and pro-vocative insight. The cross loomed as Jesus prayed in the Garden of Gethsemane. He was awaiting the arrival of His betrayer. He would face cruel suffering and merciless brutality fueled by darkness. He knew. His sweat was like drops of blood as He prayed. In the darkness, a great crowd arrived, led by Judas and armed for violence. The disciples understood what was coming: unavoidable conflict.

Peter drew his sword swiftly and struck the servant of the high priest, relieving him of an ear. Revolution! The King and the Kingdom must be defended! Here is a vivid illustration of the difference between the violence of the world and Kingdom violence. "Jesus said, 'No more of this!' And he touched his ear and healed him" (Luke 22:51).

Did you catch it? Jesus healed the ear of the man who was there to kill Him. As He was being arrested unjustly, knowing that He would be violently mocked, beaten, shamed and publicly tortured unto death, Jesus extended His hand to heal—to heal the one who was against Him.

What does Kingdom violence look like?

- The leper healed.
- The demoniacs delivered and in their right mind.
- The widow's son raised from the dead and given back to her.
- The woman at the healing conference who was deaf from birth receiving her hearing.
- The man who had a brain injury from childhood getting out of his wheelchair.
- The young woman who never felt loved transformed by the love of Jesus Christ.
- The bag boy broken, weeping and receiving Christ as Savior after being told, "You have an issue with your father, but God is going to heal you."
- Widows, orphans and the lonely invited to dinner in our homes, and consequently into relationship with Jesus to find their home.
- The sex trafficked rescued, healed and made whole in body, mind and soul.
- My husband delivered from alcohol and drug addiction, and being restored as husband and father to his family.

Kingdom violence looks like people enduring hard struggles with suffering, experiencing public reproach and affliction and having compassion on those who are imprisoned for their faith (see Hebrews 10:32–34).

Is it becoming clear? Kingdom violence looks like Jesus—a lifestyle of violent love, violent mercy, violent forgiveness, violent joy, violent grace, violent worship, violent peace and more. It is you and me being willing to sacrifice our rights, comforts, conveniences and resources to step up, speak up and bring about the Kingdom of God in all its glory—salvation, healing, intercession, deliverance, reconciliation and prophecy. It is all of His followers laying down their lives, turning their cheeks, walking the extra mile, loving their flesh and blood enemies and working to reconcile the world to God.

Finally, it is God's people rising up to take back what the enemy has stolen—broken hearts, bodies, homes, lives, cities and nations. We accomplish all of this by the blood of the Lamb, the word of our testimony and not loving our lives even in the face of death (see Revelation 12:11). We know death has lost its sting. This *is* the revolution.

More Than What We First Believed

Spiritual warfare is more than intercessory combat or deliverance ministry. Are we to engage in deliverance ministry to those in bondage? Yes. Are we to engage in intercession to combat darkness in people, regions and nations? Yes. Some in the Body of Christ, however, excuse themselves from engaging in spiritual warfare because they believe that it is a special calling or ministry that is reserved for a few. It is not. It is living the Christian life, doing good and healing all who are oppressed by the devil, wherever we find ourselves throughout our everyday lives (see Acts 10:38). We are to live a lifestyle that overcomes darkness as we hear and obey.

We are the violent in this hour, and our violence must look like Jesus. His violence looked like the Kingdom of God. He went about healing the sick, delivering those who were in bondage from demons, restoring the lost and broken, setting the outcast

116

in community and the fatherless into families, and bringing salvation to all who were around Him. He spoke out against those things that hinder others from entering the Kingdom, including religious doctrines, sin, evil, injustice, poverty and sickness. He forgave sin, loved without limits, acted in mercy and laid down His life for His friends.

Hebrews reminds us to pay close attention to what we have heard "lest we drift away from it" (Hebrews 2:1). What was the message being declared? The King and His Kingdom are here!

John asked the question, "Are you the one who is to come, or shall we look for another?" (Matthew 11:3). Jesus answered with a witness of Himself.

"Go and tell John what you hear and see: the blind receive their sight and the lame walk, lepers are cleansed and the deaf hear, and the dead are raised up, and the poor have good news preached to them" (Matthew 11:4–5). This is the revolution. This is Kingdom violence. Yes, John, Jesus is the One we have been looking for.

Summary Points

1. The Kingdom of God suffers violence. Believers and nonbelievers all suffer violence. We are to expect it.

2. When Jesus stated that the Kingdom of God suffers violence, He finished the statement with "and the violent take it by force." This expressed the connection between the Kingdom and those who would enter it. Just as there is violent opposition to His mission to overthrow Satan and his works, there is an empowered, fearless people of God who will counter the opposition as violently.

3. The first order of business is to determine the difference between the dark violence done by the enemy and Kingdom violence. Dark violence is the devil and his cohorts deceiving, enticing, seducing, murdering, stealing and destroying. Wherever you find disease, poverty, bondage, abuse and evil, the enemy is at work.

4. Jesus countered and overturned the works of darkness with every good work and miracle He performed. Jesus lived and acted in a continuous insurgency against demonic rulers, authorities, principalities and powers and their violent effects on people.

5. Opposing the plan of God is aligning with the plan of Satan.

6. Jesus' life and death demonstrated Kingdom violence.

7. Jesus healed the ear of the man who was there to kill Him. As He was being arrested unjustly, knowing that He would be mocked, beaten, shamed and publicly tortured to death, Jesus extended His hand to heal—to heal the one who was against Him. This is what Kingdom violence looks like.

8. Kingdom violence looks like Jesus. He lived a lifestyle of violent love, violent mercy, violent forgiveness, violent joy, violent grace, violent worship, violent peace and more. Kingdom violence is God's people rising up to take back what the enemy has stolen—broken hearts, bodies, homes, lives, cities and nations.

9. Spiritual warfare is more than intercessory combat or deliverance ministry. It is living the Christian life, "doing good and healing all who were oppressed by the devil" (Acts 10:38), wherever we find ourselves throughout our everyday lives. We are to live a lifestyle that overcomes darkness as we hear and obey.

Questions and Activation

1. Set some time aside for reflection. Have a journal and a Bible available. Record your answers, thoughts and anything the Lord says to you during this time.

2. Invite the Holy Spirit into your reflection time. Instead of reflecting on the violence in the world, think about the miracles of Jesus. Think and reflect on the various ways that Kingdom violence was demonstrated in the life of Jesus. Think and reflect on what a lifestyle of spiritual warfare and Kingdom violence might look like in your own life.

3. Answer the questions below.

   • How violent are you willing to be in order to rescue others who are living in darkness?

   • How violent will you be in your love for others?

   • How violent will you be in seeking first the Kingdom of God over other pursuits and desires?

- How violent are you willing to be in your willingness to forgive? Are you willing to forgive those who persecute you, betray you, do you or someone you love physical harm, steal your spouse, steal your promotion or accuse you falsely?

- How violent are you willing to be to heal the sick, prophesy or cast out demons? Are you willing to risk and fail (even publicly) fifty times, one hundred times, two hundred times or even a thousand times in order to see someone healed of sickness or disease?

Read and Meditate

Matthew 5–8

Exercise

1. Invite the Holy Spirit to bring to your mind anyone you may need to forgive.

2. Ask God to forgive you for holding onto any unforgiveness, then release forgiveness to whomever the Spirit revealed.

3. Invite the Holy Spirit to give you supernatural willingness, boldness and courage to do Kingdom violence. Ask for a gift of faith. Ask for the gift of prophecy and healing to develop in your life. Thank Him for it.

4. Ask the Holy Spirit to show you someone who needs a word of prophecy, healing or deliverance, and then go do it!

Intercession

1. Go back and read through the previous list of dark violence.

2. Invite the Holy Spirit to give you strategies for praying about each one.

3. Review the summary points, especially 7–9. Create a list of Scripture verses that reveal our Kingdom violence mission to overcome evil, to do Kingdom violence and to overcome the evil of the enemy in our spheres of influence. Then turn them into prayer points and declarations. For example,

> And he said to them, "Go into all the world and proclaim the gospel to the whole creation. . . . And these signs will accompany those who believe: in my name they will cast our demons; they will speak in new tongues; they will pick up serpents with their hands; and if they drink any deadly poison, it will not hurt them; they will lay their hands on the sick, and they will recover."
>
> Mark 16:15–18

- *Lord, You have called me to demonstrate the Gospel of the Kingdom that establishes the rule of God everywhere I go. Give me faith to do it in Jesus' name!*

- *Lord, You say that miraculous signs will happen because I believe in You and I believe You are a miracle-working God. Increase my faith, and let me see miracles in Jesus' name.*

- *Lord, You say that in Your name I will cast out demons as You did, living a life of warfare on the earth. Fill me with Your Spirit and miracle-working power. Give me*

*the faith and boldness to tell demons to leave in Jesus'
name.*

- *Lord, give me boldness to lay hands on the sick and see
  them recover. Give me prophetic revelation about the
  conditions and illnesses in the people I encounter. As I
  pray for them, heal them in Jesus' name.*

4. Commit to praying for the overthrow of each act of
   dark violence by praying and declaring Scripture over
   it for thirty days.
5. Pray for those who are afflicted and suffering because
   of the dark violence, and pray for those who are advancing the darkness by cooperating with it.
6. Ask God to awaken the Body of Christ to prayer, intercession and acts of Kingdom violence.

CHAPTER 7

War and Peace

"Peace I leave with you; my peace I give to you. Not as the world gives do I give to you. Let not your hearts be troubled, neither let them be afraid."

John 14:27

"I have said these things to you, that in me you may have peace. In the world you will have tribulation. But take heart; I have overcome the world."

John 16:33

I had stepped down from the platform at a women's conference when a woman in her midforties carrying a baby on her hip approached me.

"Pastor Kim, I want you to meet my baby." She presented me with the big-eyed child. She then proceeded to tell me a story.

When we had met before, she had been pregnant. This pregnancy occurred after she had gone through a period of infertility. The doctors, however, had discovered a tumor that was growing alongside the baby. They told her that the tumor would overtake her pregnancy, which would cause her baby to die long before birth. This tumor might even endanger her own life. It was recommended that she abort the pregnancy and have the tumor removed. She was frightened and desperate. The fact that she was over forty added to the fear and attachment. There was no more time for endless, futile medical procedures.

I was speaking at her church that week. She knew that I believed in divine healing, so she had approached me for prayer.

"When I told you what the doctors said," she said, "you prophesied to me the tumor would dissolve, and the baby would live." Then, according to her testimony, I laid my hands on her abdomen and commanded healing in the name of Jesus.

When she went to her doctor, they performed an MRI. The tumor was gone. Months later, she gave birth to the child who was now perched on her hip, giggling and drooling and reaching for my hair. The tumor was overcome by one of the least (me) doing Kingdom violence.

A Danger to Darkness

We have been exploring, interpreting and applying the revelation gained from Jesus' warning about violence done to the Kingdom. Essentially, we have been familiarizing ourselves with the war in which we find ourselves and to which we are called. We know that we are living in violent times. We now know it is a sign to us that God is moving on the earth. His movement always brings violent opposition from darkness. We also know that we are the least who are called and equipped to overcome the darkness by doing Kingdom violence. We know what Kingdom violence is and what it is not; however, there is something more we must know and receive if we are to become powerful, effectual and dangerous to the dark powers and principalities.

The truth we must comprehend and embrace is that we are unable to respond properly to violence if we do not have the peace of God in our hearts, minds, households and ministries. Where there is peace, the presence of God permeates, activates and empowers. Where there is peace, we are able to receive fresh strategies and blueprints for the days ahead. Having peace in all circumstances and situations releases the God of peace to crush Satan underneath our feet (see Romans 16:20), while we remain on task doing violence to the kingdom of darkness.

The Need for Peace

Jesus said we would experience trouble and tribulation in the world. It is to be expected.

We have already established that conflict is unavoidable. This is why He instructs us to "take heart; I have overcome the world" (John 16:33). God desires that we would have peace in the midst of these violent times. Without it, we become immobilized by fear and intimidation. My friend, minister and author of *Accessing and Releasing God's Peace*, Paul Martini once remarked to me, "Satan is a strategist and knows he doesn't have to steal your anointing, your gifts or your ministry. All he has to do is steal your peace."[1] Martini is correct.

There are over 340 passages of Scripture in the Bible that talk about peace. The words for *peace* in Hebrew and Greek occur at least four hundred times. This is important. When we look for truth in Scripture, we always want to look for what the Spirit of God has emphasized through the authors. Peace is one of those topics that has been repeated in Scripture, which means that peace is a significant subject worthy of study. We need peace.

Grace and *peace* are words that were used commonly as greeting or farewell in the culture in which the writers lived. It is a form of blessing, a hope for the days ahead. What a beautiful way to say hello and good-bye. Yet there is more.

In the gospel of John, *peace* (*eirene* in Greek) is used five times. All five are found within a six-chapter section (see John 14–20). This section contains what is called the Farewell Discourse of Jesus, which is a fancy way of saying His last sermon or message. These are His final words and instructions to His much-loved disciples.

Final words are important words. They are meant to leave an indelible mark in people's minds. Jesus is looking to the future as the cross draws near. He is looking at those who have walked alongside Him, shared a table, healed the sick, cast out demons, raised the dead and suffered rejection with Him, knowing they are about to be sent out into the world as lambs among wolves (see Luke 10:3; John 17:8). Yes, final words are important words.

The final message of Jesus that is recorded in the book of John is considered to be an assurance oracle. An oracle is a prophecy or a prophetic message about what is to come. It is divine revelation meant to give humans eyes to see the future from heaven's perspective. In this revelation, there are implications for the present as well as for the future. *Assurance* is defined as "encouragement." It inspires confidence and lends security for the future. Knowing what is ahead affords people an opportunity to prepare. Receiving assurance settles the heart and mind regarding the time ahead, and it provides stability in times of shaking, uncertainty or crisis.

This important final message from Jesus is a prophetic revelation given to His disciples to fill them with courage and confidence so that they are able to face the imminent future. Jesus does not want His disciples to be caught unprepared for what He sees coming. When He departs, He knows the disciples will have to confront a hostile world. "If the world hates you, know that it has hated me before it hated you. If you were of the world, the world would love you as its own; but because you are not of the world, but I chose you out of the world, therefore the world hates you" (John 15:18–19).

Just a few chapters after these words were recorded (the cross and resurrection having already occurred), we find that the persecution has now begun. "On the evening of that day, the first day of the week, the doors being locked where the disciples were for fear of the Jews, Jesus came and stood among them and said to them, 'Peace be with you'" (John 20:19).

The word *peace* is on the lips of Jesus three times in a space of seven verses. He is not simply greeting His disciples. He is releasing to them an impartation.

Jesus spoke to His disciples, who will become the New Testament apostles. John, through his gospel, is recounting and releasing the words of Jesus to the Johannine community. The Holy Spirit, who inspired John to write his gospel, is now speaking and releasing the words of Jesus over us, the Body of Christ. Jesus, John and the Holy Spirit knew that the Body of Christ in every age would face violent opposition from the enemy of our souls. Remember, conflict is unavoidable.

Remember also that in the midst of conflict, Jesus comes to His disciples with an impartation. "Peace I leave with you; my peace I give to you. Not as the world gives do I give to you. Let not your hearts be troubled, neither let them be afraid" (John 14:27). He also exhorts, "I have told you these things, so that in me you may have peace. In this world you will have trouble. But take heart! I have overcome the world" (John 16:33 NIV). Before we talk about the impartation, we need to talk about trouble.

The Trouble We Have

All who live in this world will have trouble. It is helpful to understand what Jesus means when He tells us that we should expect trouble. Knowing what trouble is allows us to understand the necessity of receiving the peace offered us. Much like dark violence, trouble is associated with the experience of affliction, hardship and adversity. Trouble in the world causes confusion, distress and disturbances in our minds, bodies, emotions and relationships. Trouble often looks like crises and difficult circumstances. These difficult circumstances often result in physical, mental and emotional suffering such as worry, anxiety and insecurity.

On a large scale, trouble looks like the pandemic of 2020 and the terrorist attack on the World Trade buildings in the U.S. on September 11, 2001. On a personal level, trouble looks like the day my father was fired unjustly from his job, which left our family in severe financial crisis and my dad covered in shame and depression.

Trouble also manifests as persecution against the Body of Christ:

> Indeed, in [China] . . . over 5,500 churches have been destroyed, closed down or confiscated. In India, Christian minorities are subjected to extreme persecution which manifested in at least 1,445 physical attacks and death threats against Christians in 2019. In Nigeria, in 2019, approximately 1,350 Christians were killed for their faith.[2]

Jesus spoke plainly to His disciples about the world's hatred and persecution of those who would follow Him (see John 15:18–21). The coming of Jesus exposed the sin, idolatry and corruption in the world. The light brought not only exposure but judgment. Revivals always disrupt the status quo and turn the world upside down. This process exposes sin, and it results in rage and hostility.

The first-century disciples lived in a world that was filled with violence and trouble. They experienced frustration, anger, violence and death on a regular basis. They were hated, persecuted, mocked and ridiculed. Disciples of the 21st, 22nd and 23rd centuries (and beyond) will be as well. We live in a hostile world. We will have trouble. It is not to be denied but rather to be expected.

The world that hates Jesus and His disciples is not an abstract force or concept. The world is simply a category used to represent all who oppose Jesus and the Kingdom of God, whether that takes the form of religious traditions, godless cultures, political entities or dark powers and principalities. The world as defined by Jesus is the antichrist spirit and all who are aligned with it (see John 15). As established previously, opposing the plan of God is aligning with the plan of Satan.

In such an atmosphere of hostility, it would be easy to feel defeated; however, Jesus encourages us not to allow our hearts to become troubled or fearful. We are not to be afraid, nor are we to find a place to hide and brace ourselves for the worst. We are to see a different reality. N. T. Wright, in his commentary *John for Everyone*, expounds,

> The last word isn't one of warning. It's one of good cheer. Somehow, even in the worst that is to come, the disciples can have a peace that will carry them through. This peace doesn't come from a detached, philosophical attitude. It isn't a matter of saying, "Oh well, these things happen." It isn't a shrug of the shoulders, resigning yourself to the world being a nasty place and there being nothing much you can do about it. It's a matter of standing on the ground that Jesus is going to win—indeed, that here he claims to have won already. . . . "The world" that will hate, persecute and ridicule Jesus' followers has been not sidelined, not downgraded, but *defeated*. When Jesus took upon himself the weight of the world's sin; when he burst through death itself into God's new creation; and, already, when he decisively challenged the power of corruption, decay and death in healing the cripple, the man born blind and Lazarus; in and

through all these things, he was not just proving a point but winning a victory. Not just setting an example but *establishing a new reality*.[3]

N. T. Wright, emphasis added

Indeed, we live in and from the new reality Jesus established by His life, death and resurrection. This new reality is called the Kingdom of God.

An Untroubled Heart

In Scripture, the heart is considered the governing center of man. It is the place where the will is engaged and where decisions are made that are founded on belief systems. These systems are formed by what we accept as true. This process allows a decision to become a core belief, which affects how we define reality, relationships and the world around us. These definitions become navigating principles upon which we make judgements and decisions. We act on what we believe. We have faith for what we believe.

In other words, what people believe in their hearts directs decisions that are made and the behavior that follows. When the experience of trouble is allowed to shape the heart of a believer, the Christian's new Kingdom reality will not be the basis of decisions and actions. Decisions and actions will be based on fear. Their decisions will be based on what could be personally lost, not on what might be gained for the Kingdom.

If I go to the doctor, for example, and am diagnosed with a terrible terminal illness, my belief system—my heart—will inform my decision regarding how I will respond and what actions I will take. If I believe that God heals, then in addition to treatments recommended by the doctor, I will turn to God, receive prayer and believe for a miracle as a testimony of God's grace and power. If I believe that sickness is my punishment for having lived a life that I regret, I may give in to depression and wait to die.

Jesus gives us another critical example:

> "On my account you will be brought before governors and kings as witnesses to them and to the Gentiles. *But when they arrest you, do not worry about what to say or how to say it. At that time you will be given what to say,* for it will not be you speaking, but the Spirit of your Father speaking through you."
>
> Matthew 10:18–20 NIV, emphasis added

Hear what the Spirit is saying! When Jesus instructs us not to let our hearts be troubled or afraid, He is warning us not to give in to timidity. Timidity breeds cowardice. Cowards are unwilling to act in situations of danger or opposition because of fear—fear of men, fear of the unknown, fear of loss or fear of death. It is cowardice that causes a person to deny Jesus publicly. Jesus has already told us that if we deny Him before others, He will deny us before the Father in heaven (see Matthew 10:32–33).

Those who are cowardly lose their witness; therefore, they have no place in the Kingdom of God. They cannot fight for the Gospel or the Kingdom when they are unwilling to die defending them. Cowards are listed among the faithless, detestable, murderers, sexually immoral, sorcerers, idolaters and liars as those who are condemned to eternal death (see Revelation 21:8). Strong words. Strong exhortation.

The World Is Overcome

All is never lost. Jesus has the answer to convert cowardice to courage. His answer is for us to *take heart.* We are to gather up our faith, courage and joyful confidence. We are to take hold of the new reality of the Kingdom and its King. After all, as Walter Grundmann explains, we "are in the hands of the Victor over the cosmos. Hence [we] need have no fear what the cosmos will bring."[4]

The Kingdom of God is already and not yet, meaning that it is coming to greater fulfillment every moment of every day. Jesus has already and not yet overcome the world. The final outcome is assured, and yet we live in the in-between. Because Jesus validates and affirms the truth about what we face daily, we are not asked to pretend that life is not hard and that there is no trouble. He understands we cannot control or hide from the trouble that comes. Even He suffered violently at the hands of the world. It is not to be denied, but to be expected—and it is to be overcome.

The life, death and resurrection of Christ has removed the sting of death and secured our future. He is in us, and we are in Him. He is now seated at the right hand of the Majesty on high (see Hebrews 1:3). There is more to overcome in the world. We are those who continue the mission to overcome:

> Every spirit that does not confess Jesus is not from God. This is the spirit of the antichrist, which you heard was coming and now is in the world already. Little children, *you are from God and have overcome* them, for he who is in you is greater than he who is in the world.
>
> 1 John 4:3–4, emphasis added

Jesus has gone before us and has established the future victory. In the meantime, in the midst of opposition and danger, He pours out His Spirit to empower and equip us, and He gives us peace as preparation for war.

Prepare for War

The mother of a U.S. soldier wrote, "My Marine son has a Latin saying tattooed on his arm: *'si vis pacem para bellum.'* It means,

'If you want peace, prepare for war.'"[5] The peace referred to here is the antithesis or the antidote for war. In the Kingdom of God, peace is more than the absence of conflict. It is the presence of God. It is the preparation for war.

In chapter 5, we read about Gideon, who was called by God to serve a divine purpose by overcoming the enemies of the people of God. He was being sent to war. It is in this story that we first encounter God being referred to as *peace* in Scripture.

The first time we encounter Gideon, we understand quickly that he knew he did not have what it would take to fulfill the call that had been placed on his life. He reminded God that he was the least in a family who was the least in a tribe who was the least of all. Even after Gideon's protests, God called him to be who he was created to be—the deliverer of God's people.

Gideon was not even sure who was calling him to this great task. When he offered his guest a meal, which is the hospitality of his culture, Gideon was directed to place it on a rock. In a burst of flame, the meal was consumed as a sacrificial offering. This revealed to Gideon that God Himself had visited him. He then knew with certainty this was a divine encounter, and he fell on his face in terror.

In the beginning of the story, he accused God of being a myth, absent or fickle. He suggested the miracle stories his forefathers told were just that—stories. Now, in the presence of the God of miracles, he feared being put to death. In this moment, the Lord spoke. "'Peace be to you. Do not fear; you shall not die.' Then Gideon built an altar there to the LORD and called it, The LORD Is Peace" (Judges 6:23–24). Gideon, having met the God who is peace, was now ready to be sent.

Peace Be with You

Three times in a space of seven verses Jesus says to His disciples, "Peace be with you" (see John 20:19–26). Now we know why. He saw the violence and persecution that was ahead of them. He knew what they would need to be prepared. They needed peace.

No one can stand against the enemy without giving in to fear and intimidation if he is unsure of his standing before God, or if he questions His goodness, faithfulness or power. No one can stand in the presence of dark powers and overcome the darkness without the presence of God. Before we go to war, we must have peace—both peace with God and peace from God. We must have perfect peace.

Summary Points

1. We have a need for the peace of God. Having peace in all circumstances and situations releases the God of peace to crush Satan underneath our feet. That allows us to remain on Kingdom task doing violence to the kingdom of darkness.

2. Jesus said we would experience trouble and tribulation in the world. It is to be expected, which is why He instructs us to take heart, assuring us that He has overcome the world.

3. Without peace we become immobilized by fear and intimidation.

4. In the gospel of John, *peace* is used five times in and around the Farewell Discourse of Jesus. These are the final words and instructions of Jesus to His much-loved disciples as He looks to the future with the cross drawing near.

5. The final words of Jesus are a prophetic revelation given to His disciples to fill them with courage and confidence to face the imminent future. When He departs, He knows the disciples will have to confront a hostile world. He does not want them to be unprepared.

6. Jesus warns His disciples of the trouble they will experience in the world. Trouble in the world causes confusion, distress and disturbance in the mind, body, emotions and relationships. Trouble often looks like crises and difficult circumstances that result in physical, mental and emotional suffering such as worry, anxiety and insecurity.

7. Jesus spoke plainly to His disciples about the world's hatred and persecution of those who would follow Him. The first-century disciples lived in a world filled

with violence and trouble. They experienced frustration, anger, violence and death. They were hated, persecuted, mocked and ridiculed.

8. When Jesus instructs us not to let our hearts be troubled or afraid, He is warning us not to give in to timidity. Timidity breeds cowardice. It is cowardice that causes a person to deny Jesus publicly, and Jesus has said if we deny Him before others, He will deny us before the Father in heaven (see Matthew 10:32–33).

9. Three times Jesus says to His disciples, "Peace be with you" (see John 20:19–26). He saw the violence and persecution ahead, and He knew that they needed to be prepared. No one can stand in the presence of dark powers and overcome the darkness without the presence of God. Peace is not the absence of conflict. Peace is the presence of God from His Spirit.

Questions and Activation

1. Set some time aside for reflection. Have a journal and a Bible available. Record your answers, thoughts and anything the Lord says to you during this time.

2. Invite the Holy Spirit into your reflection time. Think and reflect on how you respond most often to trouble. Think and reflect on the times when a trusted leader or friend helped prepare you to face a difficult circumstance in your life.

3. Answer the questions below.
   - Has the trouble in the world affected your faith in Jesus? If so, how?
   - What kind of trouble intimidates you and causes you to respond in fear and timidity?

- How have you experienced the peace of God in crisis?
- How has the presence of God enabled you to deal with trouble in the world?
- Are you ready to be sent into the world with a Gospel that disrupts the status quo, stirs up opposition and incites violence?

Read and Meditate

2 Timothy 1:6–9; John 14:27; 20:19

Exercise

Therefore I remind you to stir up the gift of God which is in you through the laying on of my hands. *For God has not given us a spirit of fear, but of power and of love and of a sound mind.* Therefore do not be ashamed of the testimony of our Lord, nor of me His prisoner, but share with me in the sufferings for the gospel according to the power of God, who has saved us and called *us* with a holy calling.

2 Timothy 1:6–9 NKJV, emphasis added

We now know the Kingdom of God suffers violence, which means that when a move of God—a revival, an awakening or a visitation, whatever term you like best—starts to manifest on the earth, there is violent opposition. Jesus told us to expect trouble. Conflict, we have discovered, is inevitable. We are being prepared to be sent by Him out into the world to do Kingdom violence. We get to participate in the move of God. Are you ready?

The exodus of the people of God from slavery in Egypt was a revival movement. It was a supernatural move of God that began with a miraculous deliverance. The people, however, failed to enter into the fullness of the prophetic promise and inheritance. At Mount Sinai, the people received their identity and mission; however, the mission they were sent to accomplish failed because fear and intimidation ruled the day. When they heard about the enemy that they would have to face, they became cowards. They feared for their lives and avoided the conflict.

In the next chapter, you will receive an impartation of the peace of God. In this moment, however, we will deal with fear and having a poverty mind-set. Paul says we have not been given a spirit of fear but of power, love and a sound mind (see 2 Timothy 1:7). You and I have been given the Spirit of God, and with that comes His courage, boldness, confidence and miracle-working power. We have been given His love, both for ourselves and for others. We have also been given His sound mind. We have been empowered to think God's thoughts with the mind of Christ. We have not been given a spirit of fear, which is one of the major differences between a poverty mind-set and a Kingdom mind-set.

The Israelites were rescued miraculously from Egypt. They were sent out to advance God's agenda in the Promised Land after having been slaves for four hundred years. They had a poverty mind-set. Whatever possessions, power or security they had gained, they were afraid to lose.

A poverty mind-set is based in fear. When a person operates from a poverty mind-set, they make fear-based decisions. Fear-based decisions focus on what might be lost, what might fail or what might go wrong. When the trouble of this world infects the heart and mind of a believer fear is allowed to take hold. Those fears include the fear of peers, fear of the future, fear of failing, fear of the unknown, fear of loss and fear of death.

A Kingdom mind-set, on the other hand, makes decisions based on what might be gained. Decisions are based on the knowledge that Jesus not only has power and authority but also gives that power and authority to us. In fact, all that He has He gives to us. When we follow His Word, obey His commands and go where He wants, He backs us up. Fear, timidity and cowardice will keep us from making decisions in alignment with who God is and with what God says.

Prayer

Father, I come to You in the name of Jesus confessing that intimidation has caused me to fear, falter, shrink back and turn away from what You have called me to do. Forgive me for thinking that I am inferior to the enemy or that I am powerless to meet and defeat him. Forgive me for thinking that I have been left alone. I had forgotten that I am loved and forgiven by You because of the cross and the shed blood of Christ. I have, therefore, been made right with You. I had forgotten that You have overcome the world. Because of that knowledge, I do not need to give in to fear, intimidation, anxiety or panic. I declare that I am a child of God who is filled with the Holy Spirit and who is empowered by God for battle. You have not given me a spirit of fear. I refuse, reject and rebuke a spirit of fear and intimidation. I come out of agreement and alignment with fear and intimidation and ask You to forgive me for times when I have cooperated with that foul spirit of the enemy. I now take authority over that spirit, in the name of Jesus and by the blood of the Lamb, and I break its power over my life. I command it to leave me and not return. Holy Spirit, come and fill me with boldness and fortitude. I receive from You a sound mind. Heal me and cleanse my mind from a poverty mentality. Replace it with a Kingdom mind-set. I declare from this time on that I will think and make decisions with the mind of Christ, and I will be ready to gain ground for the Kingdom of God. Thank You, Lord Jesus, for Your faithfulness to me. Thank You for giving me the gift of the Spirit. In Jesus' name, Amen.

CHAPTER 8

Perfect Peace

"Every leanness is broken by His presence."

Karyn Roy Smith

"Peace be with you. As the Father has sent me, even so I am sending you."

John 20:21

The streets were rough, the air was pungent and close, and dense graffiti marked our route. The church grounds were barricaded to prevent violation. Still, people gathered, eager for the presence and word of the Lord. They had fasted and prayed together for forty days, asking God to move in revival in their church and on the streets. The scene was not only heartwarming but also convicting. It was striking to see that the hunger of the believers outweighed the inconvenience they experienced.

Worship began. Young people in matching attire appeared on the platform to offer their gift of dance to the Lord. What appeared to be moms and dads offered instrumental background. It was not at all polished, but it was powerful. As the tempo changed, the people began to lift up a song that has long been a favorite of mine with words that declare how we want to see His face.

Unexpectedly, a group of about twenty preteens gathered directly in front of me. They clasped their arms together and began jumping, twirling and shouting the lyrics. The Spirit of God fell upon me with trembling and prophecy. An urgency gripped my heart to seize the moment for a move of God.

I searched frantically for the pastor. I was a guest in his house, so I needed permission from him to take charge of his service. When permission was granted, I stepped up to speak. A hush fell in the room as the atmosphere was pregnant with anticipation.

"The Holy Spirit wants to minister to the children," I said tenderly. "Will all of the children 25 and under come to the platform? Quickly, now come." A river of forty to fifty children ages 4 to 25 streamed to the front.

I prophesied over them collectively, and then I invited the Holy Spirit to come upon them in power. The Spirit began to fall on them. A wave of the Spirit's presence that began in one corner moved across the room. Several fell to the floor under the power of God. Some began weeping and trembling while others started laughing. Standing next to me was a nine-year-old girl who was staring into heaven with tears running down her face. She did not move, and it seemed as if she was oblivious to all that was happening around her. Her father stood behind her weeping with joy because of the encounter with the living God that she was having.

A six-year-old stood in front of me, eyes wide with fright. I asked her if she was afraid, and she confirmed that she was. I asked her what she was afraid of, not wanting to assume or put words in her mouth. She answered that she had never before felt what she was feeling, and she did not understand what was happening. She lifted her arms and hands to show me that they were visibly shaking. She said she could not help it or stop it. She told me she felt as if she was going to fall down and that her heart was burning.

I smiled and got down on my knees in front of her. I explained to her in a gentle voice what she was experiencing, and I reassured her that she could trust God and the Holy Spirit. I asked if I could lay hands on her and pray, and she nodded. The moment I put my hands on her the trembling stopped. She fell limp into my arms under the power of the Spirit. I saw that her eyes were moving in ways I have seen before when people have been experiencing supernatural vision.

The youth pastor came forward. He was weeping as he witnessed the Lord touching the children he loved and served. As I prayed and prophesied over his life and leadership, he shook and jerked with what he later described as waves of electricity.

Three days later, I received a message from him. He relayed that since we had gathered, God had been performing miracles and had brought healing to the violent streets that surrounded their church through the children who had been touched during our meeting. These were the first fruits of revival.

World Peace

In chapter 7, we learned that people cannot stand against the enemy without giving in to fear and intimidation if they are unsure of their standing before God. They cannot stand firmly if they question His goodness, His faithfulness or His power. No one can stand in the presence of dark powers and overcome the darkness without the presence of God. We have established that peace is part of the preparation for war. Before we go to war, we must have peace—both peace with God and peace that we have received from God.

Jesus said, "Peace I leave with you; my peace I give to you. Not as the world gives do I give to you" (John 14:27). He made a clear distinction between the peace He gives and the peace the world gives. We must also.

As a little girl, I can remember waiting with excitement to watch the Miss America or Miss Universe pageants on television. Every year during the interview segment when the contestants were asked what they would like to accomplish during their reign if they won, one or more would predictably say, "World peace." By this, they meant they would like all people in the world to live in peace and harmony without war. Remarkably, however, this lofty and appealing vision was never accompanied by any type of strategy. It was obviously more of a ploy to gain favor than it was an attainable goal.

Jesus never promised world peace. In fact, what He promised was tribulation and trouble in the world. The world can offer peace merely as a politically correct and polite greeting. World peace is not possible as long as sin, sickness and Satan are in the world. Only Christ, the Savior of the world, can offer the gift and experience of peace.

A brutal counterfeit was manifesting in the world when God sent His only Son to bring divine, eternal salvation and peace to all humanity. World peace in the first century was defined by *Pax Romana*, which is Latin for "Roman peace." It was established by Caesar Augustus.

The ancient world worshiped at the feet of their kings. They believed that salvation came though political and military power. "The [imperial] cult stems from the career of Augustus who after Actium in 31 BC established the *Pax Romana*. . . . He was commonly addressed as *sōtēr*,"[1] meaning both the savior of the world and the son of God. He was their god and king.

World peace, according to Rome, was offered by the so-called savior of the world. The peace he offered was secured by military force, political intrigue, brutality, bloodshed and oppression. Ironically, Augustus, as their new god, vowed to give all people new life in a world that would be marked by the absence of death and violence, all the while enforcing his will by murdering any who refused to submit. While history shows that Rome did experience peace under the *Pax Romana*, theologian Peter Bolt points out that "ultimately, these new gods did not seem to make much of a positive difference to the world under the shadow of death. . . . Despite the rhetoric, the people had been forsaken."[2]

It should be easy to make the distinction by now. Jesus, who is the true Son of God and Savior of the world, is nothing like Rome's god-king Augustus. Similarly, the peace Jesus gives is nothing like Roman peace. A counterfeit is never really like the real thing.

Earlier, we assessed the Jewish expectations of a militaristic Messianic King. Jesus refuted these ideations. He did not come into the world as a military or political dominant. He came as the suffering servant (see Isaiah 53). He did not come to crush but to be crushed. He did not come to kill but to be killed. He did not come to judge but to bear the weight of judgment for the sin of all humanity. He did not come to seek glory but to glorify the Father through self-sacrificing humility, suffering and love.

Mark Keown highlights the stark contrast:

He dies in this way to show humanity a new way—*the* Way. . . . Unlike Augustus, who established the *Pax Romana* through military force, he comes to establish the *Pax Dei* (the peace of God), not through violent overthrow, but through being seemingly defeated and yet triumphing over death as *Christus Victor*. He is a miracle worker who heals and feeds people, the ultimate benefactor who serves his people and the world without discrimination—not a despot who rules through fear and favor.[3]

War and Peace

There are no miracles without an impossible situation. There is no resurrection without a death. There is no peace without conflict.

The first mention of peace in John's gospel is found within Jesus' Farewell Discourse to His disciples as He makes His way to the cross (see John 14:27). He tells them that the world will hate them, persecute them and cause them to suffer. They will receive confirmation of these things in a short while when they witness Jesus suffer rejection, persecution, injustice, physical violence and death as He was nailed to the symbol of their hatred. There will be no peace given by the world that could comfort and secure them. There is only trouble.

There is, however, a peace that Jesus gives. It is His parting gift to His followers embodied in the Holy Spirit who will be their helper, guide and comforter. The Holy Spirit will enable them to stand steadfastly and give witness in the face of violence when He is gone. In other words, this peace is not the absence of conflict but the very presence of God by the agency of the Holy Spirit secured in the shed blood of Jesus as the guarantee. The resurrection seals the covenantal deal.

The first mention of peace in John is proleptic. The third mention of peace in John is an impartation. The violence Jesus had seen coming had begun. The disciples were huddled together behind closed doors with the trauma of the cross still fresh in their minds, their dreams of revolution shattered and their lives now in danger as they were sought by those who put Jesus to death. They were afraid.

Suddenly, Jesus came into the room. The cross and resurrection were finished. He had given His life to overcome the last enemy: death. All authority had been rent violently from darkness and had been relinquished to Him in a stunning reversal of power. The resurrection had changed everything. The tables had been turned on Satan.

Yet the world remained in darkness. The mission was not complete. Whom shall He send? The simple answer was His disciples. Though they had followed Him in life, they had scattered in His death. They had fled to avoid being identified with Him and suffering His fate, and they were hiding in fear. In order for them to be sent out on mission, something more would be required.

"Peace be with you" (John 20:19). Once they understood it was Jesus who had come into their midst miraculously, He said again, "Peace be with you. As the Father has sent me, even so I am sending you" (John 20:21).

Before He sends, He gives. Peace is the prerequisite for the sending. Peace would enable them. Peace would keep them. Peace would secure them. Peace would reassure them. Peace would give them courage. Peace would make them fearless. All would be well with their souls in the midst of crisis, chaos and danger. "He breathed on them and said to them, 'Receive the Holy Spirit'" (John 20:22).

When man received the breath of God in the Garden of Eden, he became a living being. Adam received new life by the breath. By the breath of God through Jesus there is new and regenerated life for all who receive. The breath comes from the Spirit of God who affects regeneration so completely that a person can be called born again or a new creation.

With the breath comes the gift of life and peace (see Romans 8:6; 14:17). With the Holy Spirit also comes the power to witness faithfully and fearlessly. The disciples were told to wait in Jerusalem and be clothed fully with power by the Spirit.

Jesus' mission is waiting fulfillment. For that to happen, all disciples will need both power and peace.

The Peace of Christ

Peace is the sum of all the blessings that are associated with the presence of God.[4] The Old Testament word for *peace* is the Hebrew word *shalom*. The New Testament word for *peace* is the Greek word *eirene*. The gift that Jesus gives is His own peace—the *eirene* of Christ, the *shalom* of God. It is the deepest sense of well-being in relationship to God, ourselves and others. It is a sense of wholeness, completeness, safety and security that disturbances and conflict cannot change.

Jesus lived in constant conflict, and yet He was at peace. When He was confronted, tested and tempted by Satan in the wilderness, He was hungry but at peace. When He was criticized, misunderstood and rejected, whether for having questionable parentage, eating with sinners or healing the sick on the Sabbath, He was at peace. When He was cursed, slandered, judged and condemned for being a drunkard, for claiming God as His Father or for being demonically inspired, He was at peace. When He was accused falsely, arrested, brutalized, mocked and nailed to a cross, Jesus not only held His tongue but also held His peace.

Whatever the circumstances, Jesus never changed the message to defend Himself. He never compromised with political correctness, cultural dictates or religious traditionalism. He spoke the truth even when it stirred violent opposition against Him, even in the face of death. He never gave in to the fear of man, the fear of the unknown, the pressure to perform or the pressure to conform. He never retaliated or felt sorry for Himself. He never quit. He lived and ministered with an abiding, perfect, supernatural and violent peace. This peace He imparts to us.

Perfect and Violent Peace

As the Body of Christ, peace is our inheritance. Jesus has given us reconciliation with God, a King who has an eternal Kingdom and a family of faith in every nation. We are no longer strangers or aliens, but fellow citizens with all the saints. Once we were far off, but Christ has brought us near (see Ephesians 2:13–17). This is our peace. It is Christ—the true Savior of the world, the Son of God, the Holy Spirit bearer and bestower. Christ, the Prince of Peace, is in us by the agency of the Spirit.

The peace of Christ enables us to walk in God-given authority and to stand, immovable and unwavering, rooted and grounded in Jesus while the world shakes and trembles. We know that our eternity is secure, our authority is sure and God is on our side. With this peace, we are sent into the world to do Kingdom violence in the war against darkness. The key to facing opposition fearlessly is peace. The peace of Christ is more powerful than the violence around us.

We are those who are described in Isaiah's song:

> How beautiful upon the mountains are the feet of him who brings good news, who publishes peace, who brings good news of happiness, who publishes salvation, who says to Zion, "Your God reigns." The voice of your watchmen—they lift up their voice; together they sing for joy; for eye to eye they see the return of the LORD to Zion. Break forth together into singing, you waste places of Jerusalem, for the LORD has comforted his people; he has redeemed Jerusalem. The LORD has bared his holy arm before the eyes of all the nations, and all the ends of the earth shall see the salvation of our God.
>
> Isaiah 52:7–10

Paul references the above passage when he speaks about the call of all believers to go into the world to proclaim the Gospel (see Romans 10:14–15). The gospel of peace is the Gospel of the Kingdom, which the disciples were instructed by Jesus to announce from village to village as they went about healing the sick and casting out demons (see Matthew 10:1–7).

After the death and resurrection, the disciples were sent out with peace and the power of the Holy Spirit to fulfill Isaiah's prophetic song. They were sent into the world to display the power of God's rule and reign over every demonic enemy, over all sin and over every sickness. They were sent to proclaim the peace of God that is now available through Christ the Lord.

Peace for the body. Peace for the mind. Peace for the soul. Now it is our turn.

Peace after Trauma

She was nervous and skittish. Her eyes darted this way and that way and avoided contact with mine. She was a beautiful young woman who had waited in line for over an hour to receive prayer from me. I asked how I could pray for her. Many before her had "female problems," such as infertility, polycystic ovaries or endometriosis.

She leaned in close and in a near whisper began to describe the physical and sexual abuse she had suffered. The problem that she was asking me to pray for was her inability to be intimate physically with her boyfriend. Each time they were together and began to get physical, her body and mind recoiled. She shared that she was afraid she would never be able to marry or have a family.

My heart broke for this beautiful young woman. I guessed that she did not have a personal relationship with Jesus since she approached me, a minister of the Gospel, wanting me to fix her inability to engage freely and joyfully in fornication. This assessment was not for the sake of judgement or condemnation but for the benefit of recognizing where her real need was. I could certainly pray for healing or cast out a demon, but without Jesus, how could she find peace in the aftermath of abuse?

I began to minister to her bruised and battered heart. Some of her fidgeting began to diminish. When I asked her to look me in the eye and hold my gaze, I was asking of her a great feat of strength. The fear was palpable. It was a demon. When I clasped her hands in mine and lifted them to my chest, she began to melt into me like a young daughter in the arms of her mother. I spoke to her of Jesus, the man who was acquainted with grief, sorrow, suffering and abuse. I spoke of peace. The desperation in her leapt up in hope.

As she received Christ as her Lord and Savior, the demons began to manifest and leave her with twisting and trembling. She was forgiven. Then she forgave. Together, we addressed the trauma in her body, memory and emotions. In prayer, we called on the power of the Holy Spirit to heal, fill and displace every thought, dream and picture that had been associated with her abuse. It took precious time. She was worth it. The anxiety, fear and tremors were gone. Her eyes were clear, steady and smiling. Her body was at ease. I told her that Jesus had set her free, and I asked how she felt.

She thought for a moment and then said, "I feel . . . peace."

How beautiful.

1. Jesus made a clear distinction between the peace He gives and the peace the world offers.

2. Jesus never promised world peace. He promised tribulation and trouble in the world. World peace is not possible as long as sin, sickness and Satan are in it.

3. World peace in the first century was defined by the *Pax Romana* that was established by Caesar Augustus. Rome's world peace was secured by military force and political intrigue, brutality, bloodshed and oppression.

4. The first mention of peace in John's gospel is found within Jesus' Farewell Discourse to His disciples as He makes His way to the cross.

5. Jesus tells His disciples that the world will hate them, persecute them and cause them to suffer. There will be no peace given by the world—only trouble.

6. Peace is the parting gift Jesus gives His followers. It is embodied in the Holy Spirit who will be their helper, guide and comforter. His peace will enable them to stand steadfastly and give witness in the face of violence when He is gone. This peace is not the absence of conflict, but the very presence of God.

7. The gift of peace Jesus gives is His own—the *eirene* of Christ, the *shalom* of God. It is the deepest sense of well-being in relationship to God, to ourselves and to others. It is a sense of wholeness, completeness, safety and security that is impermeable to disturbance and conflict.

8. The peace of Christ enables us to walk in God-given authority. It allows us to stand immovable and unwavering as we are rooted and grounded in Jesus while the world shakes and trembles. We know that our eternity

is secure, our authority is sure, and God is on our side. The key to facing opposition fearlessly is peace.

9. The peace of Christ is more powerful than the violence around us.

10. The gospel of peace is the Gospel of the Kingdom, which the disciples were instructed by Jesus to announce from village to village as they went about healing the sick and casting out demons.

Questions and Activation

1. Set some time aside for reflection. Have a journal and a Bible available. Record your answers, thoughts and anything the Lord says to you during this time.

2. Invite the Holy Spirit into your reflection time. Think and reflect on the difference between the peace the world offers and the peace that Jesus offers. Think and reflect on the peace Jesus exhibited throughout His earthly ministry, during His arrest and during His crucifixion.

3. Answer the questions below.

   - Do you have the kind of peace Jesus gives?
   - How would your life be different if you possessed the peace of Christ?
   - How would your words and responses change if the peace of Christ invaded your heart and mind?
   - Do you want His peace?

Read and Meditate

Romans 15:13; Isaiah 26:3; Mark 4:39; Colossians 3:15; Philippians 4:6–9; Ephesians 2:14–16; Isaiah 9:6; Psalm 46:10

Exercise

We need an encounter with the Prince of Peace by the power of the Holy Spirit, and Jesus wants to give you His peace right now.

1. Invite the Holy Spirit to come upon you in His manifest presence.
2. Be still. Know that He alone is God.
3. Repent of the times that you have taken your life into your own hands and attempted to be your own god.
4. Recommit your life into His hands and tell Him He is worthy of your trust, attention and time.
5. Make a fresh commitment to trust Him.
6. Ask the Lord to fill you with the peace of Christ.
7. Wait on Him, and become aware of His presence and His peace coming upon you.

Pray

Put your hands out in front of you in a posture of receiving. Open your heart by faith.

Come, Holy Spirit. Sweep over my mind and my heart. Father, in the name of Jesus, I still my anxieties and worries, and I acknowledge Your goodness, Your kindness, Your faithfulness, Your mercy, Your forgiveness and Your desire to give me the gift of Your peace. I ask You to remove my burdens. I invite Your peace into the places in my heart, mind and body where there has been suffering, where there is shame, where there is confusion, where there has been fear and intimidation and where there is panic and anxiety. I come out of alignment and agreement with anxiety, worry, panic, unbelief and distrust in the name of Jesus. I take authority over the spirit of anxiety, worry and panic, and I cancel the assignment of the enemy against me. I take every thought captive unto Jesus Christ in the name of Jesus. I let every fearful thought go. I silence the voice of the enemy in Jesus' name. I silence the voice of my flesh in Jesus' name. Come, Holy Spirit, and fill every crack and crevice. I honor You, Lord Jesus, as Prince of Peace. Come and make Yourself known to me, in me and through me as the Prince of Peace. I ask for, and by faith I receive, Your peace in my body, mind, soul and spirit. Come fill me with Your peace. In the midst of troubling circumstances, Jesus, I ask that You shod my feet with the gospel of peace. I want to stand rooted securely in You as I face opposition and persecution. I will not be moved. Prince of Peace, come and fill me with Your peace. In Jesus' name, Amen.

CHAPTER 9

Death Has Lost Its Sting

"Death is swallowed up in victory. O death, where is your victory? O death, where is your sting?"

1 Corinthians 15:54–55

"*Revival comes from heaven when heroic souls enter the conflict determined to win or die—or if need be, to win and die! The kingdom of heaven suffereth violence, and the violent take it by force.*"

Charles Finney, emphasis added

When the Lord told me that I should go to seminary, I was stunned. I had to look up the word *seminary* in a dictionary to find its meaning. At the time, I was serving on staff at a small, local church. I had not been to school in a dozen or more years. I had no Bible college background, and I was a mom of three teenagers. Obediently, however reluctantly, I made an appointment to speak to the admissions director at the seminary. She asked a lot of questions.

No, I did not have a completed bachelor's degree.

Yes, I was in full-time ministry.

Yes, I was older than *that*.

No, I did not know about their special student program. Evidently, seminaries hold a few spots for those who do not have a bachelor's degree but who meet age and ministry experience requirements. At the time that I inquired, they had no availability.

"Kim, we may be able to place you in two to three years when the current special students graduate."

Relieved, I drove home. Three weeks later, I was sitting in my first seminary class. One of those special students had dropped out, and the admission director felt that the Lord had chosen me to take his place. It was sudden, and it disrupted everything in my life, including my expectations.

In seminary, everything I thought I knew was shaken to its core. I thought I knew who God was and what He would do. I thought I knew what I believed. I soon discovered that everything I thought that I knew I really did not, and what I did not know was a vast ocean. It was not at all what I expected. God was at work bringing a breakthrough in my thinking and ministry.

May this be your seminary moment.

The Human Experience

I doubt that it is shocking news that suffering is part of the human experience. Suffering is not a respecter of persons regardless of age, education, socioeconomic status or religious affiliation. Pain is a common denominator and is a shared experience among humans; however, not all suffering is the same.

Suffering is an ongoing state of pain, distress or hardship. It can be the result of many types of circumstances and situations. According to the *Dictionary of Biblical Imagery*, there are

157

three types of suffering that are dealt with in Scripture: puni-tive, innocent and redemptive.[1] Suffering is punitive when it is considered just deserts for mistakes or disobedience. Innocent suffering is pain and distress that is unmerited. Redemptive suffering is the type of suffering that refines, ennobles, matures and otherwise prepares the saint to be of benefit to others.

Jesus, as we have discussed previously, did not identify Him-self as a militant Messiah conqueror. He identified Himself with Isaiah's suffering servant. He was a man acquainted with grief, suffering, rejection, abandonment, misunderstanding and ultimately violence. Jesus condescended to birth in the flesh, entering into our human experience. He was tested in every aspect as we are in order to become our High Priest who is able to sympathize with our mortal struggles, sorrows and suffering (see Hebrews 4:15). Our God and Savior who is supe-rior to the angels, to Abraham and to Moses did not consider Himself too high and lifted up to experience the hardships of being human.

Jesus paid a high price to redeem us and save us from ulti-mate suffering, but at this juncture it is important that we begin to understand suffering in light of the Fall of Adam and Eve in the Garden. In other words, how much suffering is actually a consequence of fallen humanity? The world became infected with sin-sickness and demonic activity. When sin entered the world, it brought death and the reign of Satan.

The Promise of Persecution

From the beginning, this book has been explaining the way of the Kingdom. When John the Baptist questioned Jesus' identity, He explained that the inbreaking Kingdom of God will always be met with virulent and violent demonic opposition. Again, conflict is unavoidable. Suffering and persecution are to be expected, and they are an authentication of true discipleship.

Have we, the Body of Christ, forgotten this? It is a Western aberration that leaves little room for suffering as an aspect of Christian life. In fact, it seems that modern medical, technological and even religious advances have conditioned many in the Body of Christ to "regard most suffering as an intrusion on the tranquil life that they feel is their God-given due."[2] Too often, the preaching, ministry and attitudes of the Western church that have been untouched by violent persecution betray this world view.

Here is one small example. In the local Pentecostal denomination where I was maturing during the 1990s, spiritual warfare, deliverance and spiritual mapping became an emphasis. At the time I was learning about spiritual gifts, demons and prophetic intercession. Our megachurch regularly hosted a deliverance ministry.

Many of our leaders became involved in the ministry. Members would make appointments to receive deliverance, which is the casting out of demons. During the sessions, the leaders or team members ministering to the person would attempt to uncover and name the demon who was the strong man, the demons subject to the strong man and the demons subject to the demons who were subject to the strong man, etc. At times, the ministry was incredibly effective.

After a while, however, I observed something disturbing. The ministry of deliverance became something more than freedom from demonic bondage. People seemed to think if they prayed all the *right* prayers, made all the *right* declarations, bound all the *right* demons and broke all the *right* curses that all suffering, pain and personal responsibility could be avoided. It became akin to salvation by works.

While there is substantial merit to effective spiritual warfare, intercession and declaration, it is still true that conflict, suffering and persecution are unavoidable. As Christians, suffering is to be expected as part of the call to follow Jesus. Listen to the following Scriptures (emphasis added):

Indeed, *all who desire to live a godly life in Christ Jesus will be persecuted*, while evil people and impostors will go on from bad to worse, deceiving and being deceived.

2 Timothy 3:12–13

When they had preached the gospel to that city and had made many disciples, they returned to Lystra and to Iconium and to Antioch, strengthening the souls of the disciples, encouraging them to continue in the faith, and saying that *through many tribulations we must enter the kingdom of God.*

Acts 14:21–22

For it has been granted to you that for the sake of Christ you should not only believe in him but also suffer for his sake, engaged in the same conflict that you saw I had and now hear that I still have.

Philippians 1:29–30

"*Do not fear what you are about to suffer.* Behold, the devil is about to throw some of you into prison, that you may be tested, and for ten days you will have tribulation. *Be faithful unto death*, and I will give you the crown of life. He who has an ear, let him hear what the Spirit says to the churches."

Revelation 2:10–11

"*Then they will deliver you up to tribulation and put you to death, and you will be hated by all nations for my name's sake.* And then many will fall away and betray one another and hate one another. And many false prophets will arise and lead many astray. And because lawlessness will be increased, the love of many will grow cold. But the one who endures to the end will be saved."

Matthew 24:9–13

"Blessed are those who are persecuted for righteousness' sake, for theirs is the kingdom of heaven."

Matthew 5:10

But *recall the former days when, after you were enlightened, you endured a hard struggle with sufferings, sometimes being publicly exposed to reproach and affliction, and sometimes being partners with those so treated. . . .* Therefore do not throw away your confidence, which has a great reward. For you have need of endurance, so that when you have done the will of God you may receive what is promised.

Hebrews 10:32–36

And *when they had called in the apostles, they beat them* and charged them not to speak in the name of Jesus, and let them go. Then they left the presence of the council, *rejoicing that they were counted worthy to suffer dishonor for the name.*

Acts 5:40–41

For this is a gracious thing, when, mindful of God, one endures sorrows while suffering unjustly. For what credit is it if, when you sin and are beaten for it, you endure? But if when you do good and suffer for it you endure, this is a gracious thing in the sight of God. For to this you have been called, because *Christ also suffered for you, leaving you an example,* so that you might follow in his steps

1 Peter 2:19–21

Beloved, *do not be surprised at the fiery trial when it comes upon you to test you, as though something strange were happening to you. But rejoice insofar as you share Christ's sufferings,* that you may also rejoice and be glad when his glory is revealed. If you are insulted for the name of Christ, you are blessed, because the Spirit of glory and of God rests upon you.

1 Peter 4:12–14

The Spirit himself bears witness with our spirit that we are children of God, and if children, then heirs—heirs of God and fellow heirs with Christ, *provided we suffer with him in order that we may also be glorified with him.*

Romans 8:16–17

Therefore *we ourselves boast about you in the churches of God for your steadfastness and faith in all your persecutions and in the afflictions that you are enduring.*

2 Thessalonians 1:4

Where do we find hope in such things? In Jesus. Though He was God, He humbled Himself and was obedient to the point of death. After His death, He was exalted and glorified so that at His name every knee will bow and every tongue will confess that Jesus Christ is Lord of all. We shall be glorified with Him.

Remember, too, all that we have learned up to this point. The violence and persecution we are experiencing in the world is a sign to us of the advancing Kingdom of God. None of it is a surprise to God. Jesus expected it for Himself, and He knew we also would face trouble, tribulation and violence in the world; therefore, He made every provision available to us for such times by pouring out His Spirit.

What we concluded in chapter 8 is worth repeating here. We are in Christ, and Christ, the Prince of Peace, is in us by the agency of the Spirit. The peace of Christ enables us to walk in God-given authority to remain standing, immovable and unwavering, rooted and grounded in Jesus, while the world shakes and trembles. We are able to do this because we know that our eternity is secure, and our authority is sure. God is on our side. The peace of Christ is more powerful than the violence around us.

162

Mount Up

In the book of Matthew, Jesus, the Prince of Peace and suffering servant, seems to make a declaration of war. "Do not think that I have come to bring peace to the earth. I have not come to bring peace, but a sword" (Matthew 10:34). Wait. Did Jesus not give the disciples His peace? Yes. Jesus is explaining again that there will be no peace in the world because the Kingdom of God suffers violence.

Earlier in Matthew, Jesus commissions His disciples. He gives them authority over demons and disease, and then He launches into a lengthy discourse about what they will face as they step into the call of God. He explains that they are being sent out as lambs among wolves. They will suffer persecution at the hands of people in government, in their own families and in the cities and nations in which they dwell. They will be hated, accused falsely and betrayed by those they love and trust.

Every believer will encounter persecution, violence and demonic opposition of some kind as they walk out the call of God. This is nothing new or unusual. Christian persecution has been in existence since its inception. In the U.S., the nation of my birth, Christian persecution commonly takes the form of verbal assault, social media slander, bullying, reputation sullying and wrongful termination. In other nations, Christian persecution commonly involves physical suffering or death.

In light of this, we do not ask whether or not suffering and persecution will come. It will. The question we ask is how we are to respond. Do we hide in a hovel, bury our heads in the sand or in some way disengage from life? Do we take up the sword of violence, take revenge and decide to kill or be killed? No. This is not the way of the Kingdom of God.

In the Sermon on the Mount (see Matthew 5–7), Jesus

outlines the priorities and the demands of the Kingdom of God on its citizens. Do not be angry or vengeful. Do not return evil for evil, but do good to those who mistreat you. Turn the other cheek, go the extra mile, return blessing for cursing, love your enemies and pray for those who persecute you. Forgive, give to beggars, do for others what you would like them to do for you even when they do not. Do not retaliate or demand your rights. Be the salt of the earth preserving righteousness. Be the light of the world doing ethical and supernatural good works so that God is glorified. And remember, blessed are those who are persecuted for the sake of righteousness, for theirs is the Kingdom of heaven.

Minister and author George Eldon Ladd makes a helpful comment regarding a response to persecution that preserves righteousness: "The righteousness of the Kingdom of God demands an attitude of the heart which is not motivated by selfish concerns, which does not demand even one's legitimate rights."[3] Jesus puts it another way: "Whoever does not take his cross and follow me is not worthy of me. Whoever finds his life will lose it, and whoever loses his life for my sake will find it" (Matthew 10:38–39).

Neither is saying to grin and bear it. To grin and bear it implies we can harbor resentment and anger in silence while hypocritically smiling. In doing so, we might in some small way gain smug satisfaction in thinking that we bested our human opponent. As followers of Christ, we are to lay down our lives freely for the sake of the Kingdom. We must come to the place where we are willing to pay the price even to the point of martyrdom (see Revelation 12:11).

Are you ready to die? For many of us, death has been a lifelong terror. How do we come to the place of following Christ and doing Kingdom violence against demons and darkness if it means death?

The Sting of Death

The fear of death brings bondage or enslavement. To be enslaved means not having the freedom to make choices. It means being subject to a master who holds power over you. The fear of death combined with a passion for self-preservation can drive people to make decisions that compromise their moral values and personal integrity. They do not do what they know to be right, or they feel compelled to do what they would never do under normal circumstances. They do not live in freedom. They are not truly living.

In order to truly live, which means living the life we were meant to live according to God, we must be delivered from the fear of death. The writer of Hebrews tells us this deliverance is not only possible but has already been affected by Jesus. He came in the flesh to die so that "through death he might destroy the one who has the power of death, that is, the devil, and deliver all those who through fear of death were subject to lifelong slavery" (Hebrews 2:14–15).

The devil uses the fear of death to hold people in bondage. Jesus died to set us free from death and the devil. This is good news; however, in order to understand how this dismantles the fear of death and disseminates boldness in the face of violence to us, we have to go deeper.

Behind the fear of death is a power—or sting—wielded by the devil against us (see 1 Corinthians 15:54–57). When Adam and Eve sinned in the Garden, sin and death came into the world (see Genesis 1–3). Humankind, who had been deceived by the word of the serpent, turned from faith and obedience to the word of the Lord. This process separated them from God, from themselves and from Creation. From that moment on, death and Satan reigned. Humankind seemed destined to suffer and die forever alienated, alone and tormented. Terror settled in.

But God so loved the world that He would send His Son into the world to die for all humankind (see John 3:16). When Christ died, He broke the power and penalty of sin. When He was raised from the dead by the power of the Holy Spirit, He conquered death and the power of Satan. As believers, we have received eternal life; therefore, we can shout, "Death is swallowed up in victory. O death, where is your victory? O death, where is your sting?" (1 Corinthians 15: 54–55). Death is no longer the termination of life, but rather a passageway of transfiguration to an eternal life. It is paradise in the presence of Christ (see Luke 23:43; Philippians 1:23).

Sin has been forgiven. Death has been conquered. Satan has been thrown down. The Holy Spirit has been poured out. The Kingdom of God is advancing. Jesus has ensured victory, promised eternal life, imparted His peace and issued the call and commission. Can we be anything but fearless, even in the face of suffering, violence and persecution?

Death Is Not the Worst Thing

For the Body of Christ, death is not the worst thing that can happen to us. As we have established, death is a transition to eternal life where it will have no power to harm us. The worst thing, then, is to stand before the Lord and be told, "I never knew you; depart from me" (Matthew 7:23). The worst thing is that we would be found unworthy of the call of Christ Jesus after all that He has done for us.

My great friend and colleague Dr. Alan Hawkins captures the call that is going out to each of us in this hour:

We must find the witnesses of the resurrection. We must find those who believe that hatred cannot win because it could not defeat love. We must find a people who believe that new creation is just beyond the next grave. We must find even one

166

who will love when hate has destroyed everything they found precious. We must find one who forgives while the hammer yet pounds the nail deeper. We must find one who deems the promise of a new habitation of God among us worth bearing stones against the brow. We must find what Martin spoke of as the strength to love. We must find what Nelson spoke of as impossible until it's done. We must find it today. Today is the only day we have to hear his voice. Today is the only day we have to bear the cross. Today is the only day we have to follow one who could not be destroyed by death because he did not deem killing as the release but dying.[4]

We are those who must be found. There is nothing to fear and everything to gain. It is time we join those who have gone before us and those the apostle John heard about from heaven. "And they have conquered him by the blood of the Lamb and by the word of their testimony, for they loved not their lives even unto death" (Revelation 12:11).

Let me say as plainly as I can: Christ died and conquered death so that we are no longer subject to the bondage of the fear of death that might hold us back from proclaiming fearlessly and boldly the Gospel of the Kingdom. In other words, we are now able to face death as we work to advance the Kingdom, because death has no sting, no hold on us and no fearful threat of either the unknown or annihilation. If we die, we live. If we choose to cling to this life, we have already lost it. We are now free to refuse to cling to the temporal while forsaking the eternal. It is time to choose.

Summary Points

1. Suffering is part of the human experience regardless of age, education, socioeconomic status or religious affiliation. Pain is a common denominator and is a shared experience among humans.

2. There are three types of suffering that are dealt with in Scripture: punitive, innocent and redemptive. Suffering is punitive when it is considered just deserts for mistakes or disobedience. Innocent suffering is pain and distress that is unmerited. Redemptive suffering is the type of suffering that refines, ennobles, matures and otherwise prepares the saint to be of benefit to others.

3. Jesus condescended to birth in the flesh, entering into our human experience. He was tested in every aspect as we are in order to become our High Priest who is able to sympathize with our mortal struggles, sorrows and suffering. He did not consider Himself too high and lifted up to experience the hardships of being human.

4. Much of human suffering is a result of the Fall of Adam and Eve in the Garden. It is a consequence of fallen humanity. When Adam and Eve sinned, the world came under the rule and reign of Satan. The world became infected with sin-sickness and demonic activity.

5. Suffering persecution is an expectation and an authentication of being a Christian. Persecution is expected as part of the call to follow Jesus.

6. In the book of Matthew, Jesus seems to make a declaration of war. "Do not think I that I have come to bring peace to the earth. I have not come to bring peace, but a sword" (Matthew 10:34). Jesus is explaining that there will be no peace in the world because the Kingdom of God suffers violence.

7. We should not ask whether or not suffering and persecution will come. It will. The question we should ask is how we are to respond. We are to lay down our lives freely for the sake of the Kingdom, even to the point of death.

8. The fear of death combined with a passion for self-preservation can drive people to make decisions that compromise their moral values and their personal integrity. They do what they would never normally do.

9. In order to truly live, which means living the life we were meant to live according to God, we must be delivered from the fear of death. The devil uses the fear of death to hold people in bondage. Behind the fear of death is a power—or sting—wielded by the devil against us.

10. When Christ died, He broke the power and penalty of sin. When He was raised from the dead by the power of the Holy Spirit, He conquered death and the power of Satan. Death is only a transition to eternal life where it will have no power to harm us.

Questions and Activation

1. Set some time aside for reflection. Have a journal and a Bible available. Record your answers, thoughts and anything the Lord says to you during this time.

2. Invite the Holy Spirit into your meditation time.

3. Answer the questions below.

   • Have you been born again?

   • Have you received Jesus Christ as your Lord and Savior?

- Have you confessed with your mouth and believed in
  your heart that Jesus is the Son of God who was sent
  to die in your place to pay the penalty of your sin and
  reconcile you to God?

Read and Meditate

John 3:16–17; Romans 5:6–11; 10:9–10;
1 Corinthians 15:21–22, 54–58; Hebrews 2:10–15

Exercise

Christ has delivered us from the sting of death. His life and the
life that He offers are eternal. Death is swallowed up in life. Our
mortal enemy has been defeated. As we give our lives to Christ,
we are set free from the cruel bondage to the fear of death.

Today is the day of salvation. Today you can be free. Have
you received Jesus? Receive Him now.

Pray

*Father, in the name of Your Son, I come and place my life
in Your hands. I acknowledge that You alone are God. I
acknowledge and confess that Jesus is the Christ, the Son
of God, who died for my sins so that I could be set free. I
ask You to forgive me of my sins. Wash me clean. I repent
from my old ways of doing things that are right in my eyes
but are not in Yours. I commit to walk in Your ways from
this day forward. I receive You as my Lord, Savior, Healer,
Deliverer, Redeemer and Friend. I give You my whole life
freely and willingly. Open my ears that I may hear Your*

voice. I will obey Your words and live my life, from this day forward, according to Your Word and Your will for me. I ask You to fill me with Your Holy Spirit and power to live my life in a new way. Thank You for giving Your life for me while I was still dead in my sin. Thank You for saving me and filling me with Your Spirit. Thank You for giving me eternal life. Thank You for loving me. In Jesus' name, Amen.

- Once you have received salvation, you have received eternal life. You are a new creation. The old is passed away and your life becomes brand-new.
- Tell someone about it.
- Read and study the Bible.
- Talk daily with the Lord about everything.
- Find a church community close to you that holds to the Word of God, honors the presence of God and celebrates the Holy Spirit and all of His gifts.

CHAPTER 10

We Are the Violent

Words are not enough to claim the Kingdom of God. It takes strength and courage and violence. You must violently give up all that holds you back from God. Violently turn your will over to him to do his will alone. This violence is what I pray you will come to know, for how else will you know anything of the life of the Lord Jesus?

Francois de Fenelon, *The Seeking Heart*

I was blinded by my own self-righteousness and arrogance. It nearly destroyed the opportunity God was giving me to do Kingdom violence. The experience has marked me, and each time I speak of it, I feel it as though I am still standing in the same space.

I had been invited to minister in a megachurch whose membership was in the multiple thousands. Rumors of abrupt and aberrant behavior, even abuse, due to the declining mental health of the lead pastor gave me pause. Yet I felt the leading of the Spirit to go.

A hypervigilance swept over me as I arrived. Without my noticing it, this hypervigilance came with a critical spirit. Worship began. On the platform before six thousand people, the pastor began posting feverishly to social media. I caught what he was posting out of the corner of my eye. He was inflating the numbers—not by a little, but by a huge margin. I suppose it was to impress and to protect his public appearance. I was offended immediately. In my mind it was hypocrisy. Suddenly, I did not want to be there. I felt I had nothing to give to this pastor and his church. My heart began to close its doors and hoard its love inside. I was indignant. I became stonyhearted.

With the final song of the worship set and without provocation or invitation on my part, the manifest presence of God fell upon me. I was piercingly aware of the kindness of the Lord. In sweet agony, I was brought to my knees without even one moment of consideration of the public spectacle it would be. My body shook as I wept. God opened the eyes of my heart to see beyond the sin, beyond the performance and beyond the appearances.

I knew by revelation the exhaustion, suffering and pain that the leaders who served this infirmed pastor had tolerated. Out of love and honor they had tolerated abuse, accusation and erratic behavior. A moment earlier, I had seen none of it. With His lovingkindness there came no indignation, criticism, condemnation or reproach. There was no hint of punishment or disappointment. There was only an agonizing compassion that was coupled with a desire to heal, cleanse and comfort. I was undone. It took several minutes for me to collect myself.

I had been tangibly touched by the love and kindness of the Lord. He invaded my heart in a way that I had not experienced previously. It has never left. Neither has the knowledge that I nearly missed the precious privilege of serving the people of this church with the violent love of Jesus.

The Sickness

We know humanity is sick. We know there is something terribly wrong with the culture. We see the symptoms: racism, division, violence, sex trafficking, addiction, loneliness, etc. We search for meaning and purpose, but instead find dysfunction, disappointment and disillusionment. We try to find the cure by turning to causes, social justice movements, self-esteem books and every kind of pleasure or vice to fill up what we know is lacking. We look to our political parties and candidates hoping to find justice and be rescued from poverty and bondage.

Our culture has largely become narcissistic and entitled. Narcissism is self-love—the excessive interest in one's appearance, comfort, importance and ability. It can become a pervasive and pathological pattern of grandiosity, lack of empathy and hypersensitivity to the evaluation of others. Entitlement is the belief that we are deserving of certain privileges without having to pay a personal cost for them. These attitudes and world views infect those in the culture, whether they are churched or unchurched.

In other words, the world loves only itself. Self-love cannot heal the sicknesses of humanity, because it cannot hear and respond to lament, comfort in suffering, be present in grief and loneliness, be trusted in trouble, be an anchor in hopelessness or be a bridge in division. Self-love cannot provide compassion, kindness, community or rest.

Jesus and His Gospel are the answer. We, His people, possess the cure. G. K. Chesterton, a British writer and theologian, said,

> The Saint is a medicine because he is an antidote. Indeed that is why the saint is often a martyr; he is mistaken for a poison because he is an antidote. He will generally be found restoring the world to sanity by exaggerating whatever the world neglects, which is by no means always the same element in every age. Yet each generation seeks its saint by instinct; and he is not what

the people want, but rather what the people need.... Therefore it is the paradox of history that each generation is converted by the saint who contradicts it most.[1]

We, the ones who love violently, are the antidote for a culture that is bound by self-love.

Violent Love

As was written at the beginning of this chapter, "Words are not enough to claim the Kingdom of God. It takes strength and courage and violence." Fenelon's words are the essence of what this book is about: the Kingdom of God is suffering violent demonic opposition, and we are being called out of passivity and complacency into a violent faith to advance forcefully God's agenda on the earth.

Words are not enough. Knowing this is the call is not enough. Determination and self-will are not enough. Self-denial, self-confidence and self-sacrifice are not enough. Vision and passion are not enough. In chapter after chapter, we have seen that claiming the Kingdom will require the lifestyle of Kingdom violence in which we lay down our rights, comforts, conveniences and resources. It will require that we commit to turn the other cheek, walk the extra mile and give our lives, even if it means death. Even this, however, is not enough if we do not have violent love.

Love must be the motivation and the foundation. Otherwise, the violence becomes self-serving and self-satisfying. Violent love puts to death all other lovers—the love of self, love of fame, love of success, love of money, love of power and love of pleasure. Without a violent love for God and others, I cannot deny myself or subjugate my own self-love. It is when I have a true and violent love for God that I can willingly, without rancor, lay my life down for others.

This is what Paul is saying to us in 1 Corinthians 13 when he exhorts us to love. He is speaking to the charismatic church at Corinth. In the center of a message about the supernatural gifts of the Spirit, Paul tells us to pursue love. Power is heady and dangerous. It creates celebrities, even in the Church. Love is the only way we can let go of the pursuit of reputation, pride, self-importance, fame and fortune.

Love is the greatest power. It is immunization against division, superiority and pride. It is immunization against narcissism and entitlement. Without love, Paul tells us that all that we do for the Kingdom is narcissistic (see 1 Corinthians 13:1–3). Even if I am gifted in preaching, teaching and speaking in tongues with interpretation, I am simply calling attention to myself if I do not have love. I am noise to the world. Even if I receive revelations, can prophesy with incredible accuracy, have an education, can perform miracles, can acquire wisdom and understanding of all matters, I have only attempted to make myself famous if I do not have love. I am not important in the eyes of the King and His Kingdom. Even if I give sacrificially to the point of poverty or death and I look humble to others, if I have not love, I have gained nothing for the Kingdom.

Jesus loved us violently. You can find His violent love in plain language in Isaiah 53:

> He had no form or majesty that we should look at him, and no beauty that we should desire him. He was despised and rejected by men, a man of sorrows and acquainted with grief; and as one from whom men hide their faces he was despised, and we esteemed him not. Surely he has borne our griefs and carried our sorrows; yet we esteemed him stricken, smitten by God, and afflicted. But he was pierced for our transgressions; he was crushed for our iniquities; upon him was the chastisement that brought us peace, and with his wounds we are healed. All we

like sheep have gone astray; we have turned—every one—to
his own way; and the LORD has laid on him the iniquity of us all.

verses 2–6

Love costs something. There are hundreds of passages about
love in Scripture. Many of them are hard sayings about the
difficult choices of self-denial that only come easily to those
who love violently. The violent love of Christ in and through
us is the antidote for what ails our culture. Violent love must
be the motivation that compels us to do Kingdom violence.
When we love violently as Jesus does, we are willing to pay
the cost—our very lives.

Violent Grace

Violent love is the motive. Violent grace is the faculty. Grace
is not mercy. Grace is a powerful and empowering presence
of God. This is the enablement we are given in order to do
Kingdom violence. We all have been given grace, so we are all
empowered to minister through His gifts to every place and
person to whom we are sent. This is how we all participate in
the mission of Christ.

We have been given the Spirit of God, who is the Spirit of
power and prophecy. It is the Spirit who empowers the various
gifts, services and activities that are in us (see 1 Corinthians
12:4–6). Paul tells us we have been given the grace of God,
or *charis* in Greek. Because of this, we are enriched in word
(*logos*) and knowledge (*gnosis*) and are not lacking in any gift
(*charismata*) (see 1 Corinthians 1:4–9). Paul speaks to the
division and competition among the Corinthians. This leads
him to discuss the many gifts and the one Spirit, who is the
Holy Spirit of prophecy and power. Paul concludes with the
proper exercise of those same gifts. Paul is saying that we have

177

all received God's grace, and because we have received God's grace, we cannot be possibly lacking in any gift.

For a long time, many in the Body of Christ have accepted subtle forms of cessationism or demythologization (removal of the mystery and miraculous) in their theology. This has led them to define *grace* as the goodwill or unmerited favor of God. Actually, the goodwill and unmerited favor of God is *mercy*. Grace is the empowerment of God by the Holy Spirit in which we receive His gifts and are augmented supernaturally in our capacity and potential to function in prophetic wisdom and utterance, healing, deliverance, miracles, signs and wonders.

Grace is the power of the Spirit by which we do Kingdom violence. It is how God gifts us to complete the mission of Christ. It is the empowerment that was given at Pentecost when the Holy Spirit who was promised by Father God was poured out from heaven. That outpouring was to fill the Body of Christ individually and corporately. We have received grace upon grace to do the book of Acts!

Violent grace is the enablement to do the good works of Kingdom violence: healing, deliverance and raising the dead. We were created to do them. Paul writes, "For we are his workmanship, created in Christ Jesus for good works, which God prepared beforehand, that we should walk in them" (Ephesians 2:10). These good works are not only kind, ethical and moral acts but also the mighty, supernatural words and deeds of a people who are empowered with violent grace by the Holy Spirit. They are a testimony of Jesus, as He explained after He healed a man who had been an invalid for 38 years. "For the works that the Father has given me to accomplish, the very works that I am doing, bear witness about me" (John 5:36). The healing of the invalid was a work that God had prepared beforehand for Jesus. The works bear witness of who Jesus is by signs, wonders and miracles.

The Jews were divided deeply about who Jesus was and how He could perform miracles. At the point that they were ready to stone Him, Jesus asked, "I have shown you many good works from the Father; for which of them are you going to stone me?" (John 10:32). When He asked which of the good works they were referring to, He was talking about the miraculous healings that He had performed, such as the man born blind whose sight He had restored. We see from these passages that good works are far more than ethical and moral acts.[2]

In case you are wondering if the good works that Jesus did are for us to do as well, He tells us as much. "Truly, truly, I say to you, whoever believes in me will also do the works that I do; and greater works than these will he do, because I am going to the Father" (John 14:12). Yes, we are created to do acts of Kingdom violence—which are good, ethical, moral and supernatural works—by violent grace.

As the Body of Christ, we are all called to minister in His gifts by the grace given us in the Holy Spirit. We are a prophetic community. The power of God is for everyone. We do not need to wait for a sign or special phenomenon. We need to go. We are told to go into all the world and preach the Gospel. This means that we cast out demons, heal the sick, prophecy, speak in tongues and preach the Gospel of the Kingdom (see Mark 16:15–18).

Jesus has already commissioned us to go. He has given us His Spirit and His peace. It is not actually a request—it is a command. Jesus commands His disciples, "Heal the sick, raise the dead, cleanse lepers, cast out demons. You received without paying; give without pay" (Matthew 10:8). He also commands His disciples, "Go therefore and make disciples of all nations, baptizing them in the name of the Father and of the Son and of the Holy Spirit, teaching them to observe all that I have commanded you" (Matthew 28:19–20).

To be a Christian is to be a witness—in miracle working power—to the one who is Lord over sin, sickness and Satan. To be a believer is to be a preacher of the Gospel. To be a believer is to do Kingdom violence. Do we truly believe?

Violent Faith

A man brought his demon-possessed son to Jesus' disciples, imploring them to cast out the demon. His son was suffering intensely from the cruelty inflicted upon him by the demon. The disciples could not cast the demon out or heal the boy. Jesus healed him with a simple rebuke. The boy had been suffering violence. Jesus stepped in to do Kingdom violence, and the demon had to go. The disciples asked Jesus, "Why could we not cast it out?"

The answer Jesus gave to His disciples is the answer He gives us today. "Because of your little faith. For truly, I say to you, if you have faith like a grain of mustard seed, you will say to this mountain, 'Move from here to there,' and it will move, and nothing will be impossible for you" (Matthew 17:20). Kingdom violence requires violent faith.

I was standing in a service in a foreign country getting ready to pray for people who needed healing—my first time. I had on my brave face. I figured that expressing nervousness would not add to an atmosphere of faith. Standing near the platform a line of people who were afflicted, tormented and diseased began to form.

Silently, I asked God to have mercy on me and bring a simple need into my line. I knew it was silly. After all, is any healing less miraculous than another? Still, I asked. Out of the corner of my eye I watched a man with leg braces who was assisted by his wife make his way to my line. Inwardly, I groaned.

That's too hard Lord, I prayed silently. Not only did the man still come, but all of the others backed up to allow him to go first. I did not know if I had the faith to even utter a prayer for this man, much less expect him to receive healing.

For his sake, I mustered the courage. He hobbled up close on legs that were twisted, misshapen and imprisoned in metal. He was smiling. His wife was guarded. Through an interpreter, he told me what he wanted prayer for. He had been struck with polio as a young child. The disease had ravaged his body and left him in constant pain and unable to walk without the aid of metal braces, splints and crutches. Over the years, he had accepted his deformities and had learned to function. Now as a middle-aged man he stood before me asking me to pray for Jesus to heal him. I stretched out my hand to touch his forehead lightly, and I began to pray.

"*Deus, em nome de Jesus, vem Spirito Santo.*" This means, "God, in the name of Jesus, come Holy Spirit."

Before I uttered another word, the man fell back onto the ground like a dead man. His eyes began rolling around underneath the lids.

His wife began screaming, "What have you done to my husband?" Being a former registered nurse, I did what I knew to do. I stooped down and took his pulse. It was normal. His color was good.

I then understood. He had fallen under the power of the Holy Spirit and was seeing something. He lay on the ground completely still for a good ten minutes. His eyes darted and rolled around. While he lay still, I laid hands on his legs and prayed for straightening, lengthening and healing. Nothing more happened. After what seemed like an eternity, he opened his eyes. A wide smile spread across the landscape of his pain-etched face. His wife helped him stand.

"When you touched me," he began, "I felt all the strength in my body leave me, and I was suddenly floating." He said that he did not know if he was in heaven, but he knew that he had no pain. He was filled with peace. He had no awareness of the room or the people around him. As he lay there, Jesus approached him and touched his spine. The man heard and felt something in his back move and "connect." Electricity shot from the top of his spine through the bottoms of his feet. During his time of repose, the electrical shock continued to travel up and down his body.

When he got up from the floor, he declared that he could feel his feet. In response, his wife wept openly. The man explained that when the polio had distorted his skeleton as a boy, it had caused a partial severing of his spinal cord. That process had left his legs without feeling other than constant pain. Now, however, the pain was gone, and the feeling in his legs had returned! Though not healed completely, he still rejoiced. He had tears rolling down his cheeks because of the joy of his experience with the manifest presence of God.

Meeting Jesus in the heavenly realm had stripped the years of physical suffering of their woeful commentary on his life. Jesus, not the man's suffering, would have the last word. The man lifted his arms to heaven and began to worship God and give Him glory for his healing. It was a tender and most holy moment. Then, he and his wife walked away.

Even now, tears come to my eyes. To witness the end of suffering in a person's life by the grace and power of God, whether through salvation, deliverance, healing or reconciliation, is an incredible privilege. It is sacred and holy. This miracle was the moment I knew there was something more to be had of the power of God than what I had experienced previously. This was the moment I reached out to grab hold of mountain-moving, violent faith, if only the size of a mustard seed. It proved to be the first of hundreds and thousands of healing miracles, salvations and deliverances that I would witness or participate in. To God be the glory.

Who We Are

We are the violent. We are motivated by violent love, we are empowered with violent grace, and we walk in violent faith to do Kingdom violence against dark forces that are enslaving humanity. We live a lifestyle of Kingdom violence as Jesus did.

Summary Points

1. We know humanity is sick, and that there is something terribly wrong with the culture. We see the symptoms: racism, division, violence, sex trafficking, addiction, loneliness and more.

2. The world loves only itself. Self-love cannot heal the sickness of humanity because it cannot hear and respond to lament, comfort in suffering, be present in grief and loneliness, be trusted in trouble, be an anchor in hopelessness or be a bridge in division. Self-love cannot provide compassion, kindness, community or rest.

3. We, His people who love violently, possess the cure. We are the antidote for a culture that is bound by self-love.

4. Without a violent love for God and others, we cannot deny ourselves or subjugate our own self-love. It is when we have a true and violent love for God that we can willingly, without rancor, lay our lives down for others.

5. There are hundreds of passages about love in Scripture. Many of them are hard sayings about the difficult choices of self-denial that only come easily to those who love violently. The violent love of Christ in and through us is the antidote for what ails our culture.

6. Violent love is the motive. Violent grace is faculty. Grace is a powerful and empowering presence of God. It is the enablement that we are given in order to do Kingdom violence.

7. Violent grace is the enablement to do the good works of Kingdom violence. These good works are not only kind, ethical and moral acts but also the mighty, supernatural words and deeds of a people who are empowered with violent grace by the Holy Spirit.

8. Violent faith is the vehicle for moving mountains and doing Kingdom violence. By faith and in the power of the Holy Spirit sickness is healed, demons are cast out, the dead are raised and darkness is overcome.

9. We are the violent. We are motivated by violent love, empowered with violent grace and walk in violent faith to do Kingdom violence against dark forces that are enslaving humanity. We live a lifestyle of Kingdom violence as Jesus did.

Questions and Activation

1. Set some time aside for reflection. Have a journal and a Bible available. Record your answers, thoughts and anything the Lord says to you during this time.

2. Invite the Holy Spirit into your reflection time. Think and reflect on the suffering you see in those around you—your family, co-workers, neighbors and nation. Think and reflect on the lifestyle of Jesus as He walked the earth. Think and reflect on His way of love, grace and faith.

3. Answer the questions below.
   - Have you ever been blinded by your own self-righteousness and arrogance?
   - What effect did Jesus have on those who were suffering, afflicted and demonized?
   - When was the last time you did Kingdom violence?
   - How does your understanding of love compare to the love commanded of us in Scripture as followers of Christ?

- How does the understanding of violent love, violent grace and violent faith have an impact on how you will live your life going forward?

Read and Meditate

Acts 1–3:10; Matthew 28:18–20; Mark 16:15–18; Hebrews 10:35–39; Isaiah 60:1–2

Exercise

It is not church as usual. It may seem as if the world has gone mad, but those who have eyes to see and ears to hear know we are entering an unprecedented time in which the Gospel will again be preached and practiced with power.

We are to be the violent ones who will take the darkness by force. Our violence must look like Jesus!

- Healing the sick.
- Delivering those who are in bondage to demons and darkness.
- Restoring the lost and broken.
- Placing the outcast into community and the fatherless into families.
- Bringing salvation to all—even those who have treated us unjustly, accused us falsely or persecuted us.
- Speaking out against those things that hinder others from entering the Kingdom, whether they are religious doctrines, cultural ideologies, all forms of perversion and abuse, injustice, poverty or oppression.

Jesus did violence to the kingdom of darkness through violent love, forgiveness, mercy, signs, wonders, miracles and healing. His response to John is a prophetic declaration of what God is doing right now.

Peter confirms Jesus was the King of this new Kingdom. "Men of Israel, hear these words: Jesus of Nazareth, a man attested to you by *God with mighty works and wonders and signs that God did through him in your midst, as you yourselves know*" (Acts 2:22, emphasis added).

The author of Hebrews reminds us that

> We must *pay closer attention to what we have heard, lest we drift* away from it. For since the message declared by angels proved to be reliable, and every transgression or disobedience received a just retribution, how shall we escape if we neglect such a great salvation? It was declared at first by the Lord, and it was *attested to us by those who heard, while God also bore witness with signs and wonders and various miracles and by gifts of the Holy Spirit.*
>
> Hebrews 2:1–4, emphasis added

And what was the message being declared? The blind receive their sight, the lame walk, the lepers are cleansed, the deaf hear, the dead are raised up and the poor have the Good News preached to them. As I have said before, this King and His Kingdom are more powerful than sin, sickness and Satan. God bears witness to this Kingdom with healing signs and wonders. No Church, it is not church as usual anymore.

You must hear the call of God to go.

> "Go into all the world and proclaim the gospel to the whole creation. Whoever believes and is baptized will be saved, but whoever does not believe will be condemned. And these signs

will accompany those who believe: in my name they will cast
out demons; they will speak in new tongues; they will pick up
serpents with their hands; and if they drink any deadly poison,
it will not hurt them; they will lay their hands on the sick, and
they will recover." . . . And they went out and preached everywhere, while the Lord worked with them and confirmed the
message by accompanying signs.

Mark 16:15–20

I am calling you to awaken and arise. This is your task. Jesus
has commissioned you. "Go into the world and preach the gospel to all creation."

You can no longer sit in church and say, "I don't know my
identity yet." I am telling you who you are. You are the Church
of God. You are the army of God. You are the light of the world
and the salt of the earth. You are disciples of Jesus, children
of God and co-heirs with Christ. You are filled with the Holy
Spirit who enables you for your task. You do not have to wait
to be sent to Africa. Your mission field is your family, neighborhood and city. Everywhere you go—the grocery store, the
library, your school or your workplace—people are waiting to
be healed, set free, prophesied to and brought into the Kingdom through salvation.

From this moment on, you cannot say you did not know.
You are responsible before God for what you do with your life
in light of your task.

Holy Spirit, come!

Conclusion

Of Issachar, men who had understanding of the times, to know what Israel ought to do.

1 Chronicles 12:32

From the days of John the Baptist until now the kingdom of heaven has suffered violence, and the violent take it by force.

Matthew 11:12

I t is time for us to be about our Kingdom task. In Aimee Semple McPherson's famous sermon *This Is My Task* that was preached in Angelus Temple in Los Angeles on March 12, 1939, she reminds us all, "What is my task? To get the gospel around the world in the shortest possible time to every man and woman and boy and girl!"[1] Yes, Sister Aimee, this is our task.

We have come a long way from where we began in this book, and yet we are ending where we began. We are living in violent times. The world is changing, nations are vying for power and culture is becoming more and more suspect of those who profess faith in Christ alone. The unrest and opposition we are experiencing in the world is a sign of the Spirit of God on the move. God has a plan, and it has already been enacted. We are being called to participate in this great move of God!

We have explored together the meaning of Jesus' sobering words in Matthew 11:12. The underlying thesis all along has been that the keys to prepare the Body of Christ for violent times ahead are in the answer that Jesus gives to the question of His Messianic identity and agenda.

We know that we are in a war, and as part of humanity, we are experiencing violence. It is to be expected. Jesus said to expect it. How do we respond? What does it mean for us? The answers to these questions have guided our discussion.

We looked closely at John the Baptist and his own Messianic expectations. We saw how they were not only left unmet but were also completely rejected by Jesus. As John suffered violence unjustly at the hands of a wicked leader, he was tempted to reject the One he had endorsed as Savior of the world. This is what inspired his question to Jesus.

In response, Jesus confirmed that He was changing the Messianic narrative of the nation from conquering king to suffering servant. He was calling all to open their hearts and ears to a whole new era and order. In that new era and order, which is the Kingdom of God, the followers of Jesus would be given new power and authority to overcome darkness.

Jesus came to save the lost and overcome darkness in a cosmic conflict. From the beginning, the war over the earth has raged and has affected humankind through sin, sickness and demonic afflictions. Jesus came to change those consequences and to help us see through His lifestyle the distinctions between dark violence and Kingdom violence.

Dark violence is the work of the devil and his cohorts to deceive, entice, seduce, murder, steal and destroy. Kingdom violence is a lifestyle of violent love, violent mercy, violent for-giveness, violent joy, violent grace, violent worship, violent peace and more. It is laying down our rights, comforts, conveniences and resources. It is turning the other cheek, walking the extra mile and loving even our enemies for a chance to reconcile the world to God. This is the revolution Jesus came to bring.

In chapters 7 and 8 we focused on peace. There is both war and peace in the Kingdom. To face war, Jesus gives us peace. Not just any peace, but His peace. His peace is a perfect and violent peace that prepares us to be able to stand in the day of suffering and violence. Peace is the prerequisite, because even in the midst of crisis, chaos and danger, all will be well with our soul.

Would it surprise you to know that I trembled as I approached chapter 9? In "Death Has Lost Its Sting," a short and simple theology of suffering is offered to you. Suffering, like conflict, is unavoidable. Suffering persecution is a common denominator in the lives of Christians all over the world. It has been my fear that the Western Church is not prepared to die for the Gospel. Our time is coming. The way we can face it is to know that death has been conquered by Jesus.

Finally, you received a commissioning that was proclaimed by Jesus generations ago. It was accepted by a great cloud of witnesses who are now watching to see if our generation will take up our task. I will. Will you? It will not be easy. It will be violent. I must point out one more important lesson that comes as Jesus is giving a forewarning instruction to His disciples:

> "Beware of men, for they will deliver you over to courts and flog you in their synagogues, *and you will be dragged before governors and kings for my sake, to bear witness before them and the Gentiles.* When they deliver you over, do not be anxious how you are to speak or what you are to say, for what you are to say

will be given to you in that hour. For it is not you who speak, but the Spirit of your Father speaking through you."

Matthew 10:17–20, emphasis added

Did you catch it? Jesus will use trouble and persecution as a vehicle to assist us in spreading the Gospel. We cannot give in to fear. We cannot shrink back in order to avoid conflict. In the conflict will be an opportunity to advance the Kingdom of God! There is one final question I must ask you.

How Big Is Your Gospel?

A few years back, I went to a concert of a world-renowned band. They asked their audience a question: "Do you know what time it is in the world?" Suddenly, massive clocks appeared on widescreen all over the stadium. Tick, tock. Tick, tock. Tick, tock. A moment of silence. Then the invitation to join together as one—all faiths, all people, all together to end global poverty and do social justice.

The idea given at the concert was that if we will all come together as one people with one purpose, we could end poverty and bring justice and equity to the whole world. If this is the answer, however, for bringing an end to poverty and injustice, with which group and with which ideology are we joining together with one voice to deliver true justice and equality? Socialism? Communism? Humanism? Feminism? Liberationism? Islam? Buddhism? We need to think about this.

I am not saying that movements with their pet ideologies aimed at social justice are not attempting to alleviate pain, inequality or injustice. But the question that I am posing is can any of the darkness in this world—sin, injustice, poverty or suffering—be healed and put right by any ideology or movement that is divorced from the truth of Scripture, the love of

God, the cross of Jesus and the power of the Holy Spirit? Can true justice, mercy and transformation be had without Jesus? Can we really solve the world's problems without Christ? Can unity be had by anything other than the anointing and bond of the Holy Spirit? Is this what you believe?

A few more important questions. If we end global poverty, is that enough? If we have an impact on society with new laws, and if we flood the streets with community activism, is that enough? If we rescue a sex-trafficked child or free a people from their racial oppression, is it enough? Is this the Kingdom of God? Is this the mission of Jesus? Or is there more?

The Gospel of the Kingdom not only rescues but also restores, makes whole and makes new. It is not enough to rescue children from sex trafficking. We must restore them to wholeness and keep them from hell. It is not enough to end poverty. We must restore dignity and identity. We must provide resources to fulfill the purpose for which people were created.

Only the Holy Spirit can heal the trauma and restore to wholeness those who have endured such evil. Unless people are healed and restored, how will they live truly free? We must offer them life in Christ with eternal salvation. We must restore their identity and purpose, cast out their demons and send them into the world with peace, power and authority.

We live in a secularized society that is divorcing and divesting itself from everything sacred, everything transcendent, everything Christian and everything Jesus. Yet we are created in God's image. To be truly human is to be set free from the ravages of darkness—sin, Satan and sickness. It is to be made whole and holy, regenerated in mind, body, soul and spirit. It is to be restored to relationship with God and one another.

Dark violence suspends, corrupts, ravages and kills our humanness. It intends to destroy the *imago Dei*. It inflicts murderous injury on the mind, body, soul and spirit of a human. It desires for the glory of God in us to be destroyed and divulged from all things sacred, holy and human. To be truly human is to be in Christ, us in Him, and Him in us.

Evil treats its victims as nothing more than lumps of tissue, whether in the womb or out. How else could we account for the atrocities in the world? The only cure for evil is Jesus and His Kingdom.

If social justice is divorced from Jesus, is it justice, or is it some kind of corrupted human idea and plan? Can any person, race or society become truly human after they have experienced violent abuse, trauma and atrocities if they are deprived of the redemptive power of God? Without Jesus, can they be restored not only to safety and provision but to life, identity, purpose and glorious eternity?

We have been entrusted with the Gospel of the Kingdom, whose mystery is the creation of one new man—no more Jew or Greek, slave or free, male or female. We are identified in Christ as God's children and not by our cultural, sexual, political, ethnic or ideological identities. The Kingdom and its King unify us by the power of the Spirit.

We are the violent. We are bringers of the Kingdom of God who are sent to establish the rule and reign of Jesus and His will on the earth. We are a supernatural people who are empowered not only to end global poverty, sex trafficking and division but also to start a revolution of cultural transformation on every level and in every aspect of society until the kingdoms of this world become the Kingdom of our God!

Again. I ask you. How big is your Gospel? It is surely a Gospel of rescue. Yet, in its fullness, it is a Gospel of violent power that is able to redeem. No, Jesus did not only come to end poverty. He came to end poverty, sickness, bondage, sin, fear, sex trafficking, degradation, racism, greed, abuse and so much more. He came to bring heaven to earth. Healing, deliverance, restoration, reconciliation, redemption and salvation come from the Lord.

He came to bring God's program of new creation. He came to make all things new, whole, complete and original in purpose and identity. When a society becomes infected by Kingdom and widespread revival, the culture begins to shift to embrace divine truth. Light invades darkness. Poverty, sickness, crime, lawlessness and racism are displaced. This is the inevitable result when the violent take the Kingdom into the world by force.

We are living in a powerful time. God is up to something big in the world. This is a time of shaking, breakthrough and violence. There is warfare in the heavens over who will rule the earth. The end has already been decided, yet the counterfeit kingdom of darkness is moving violently on the earth. The enemy is attempting to strike fear into the hearts of all who refuse to bow down to the gods of this age. Intimidation and violence have always been the name of the enemy's game.

We now know violent times are a sign to us. They are a sign of a fresh awakening and the next coming wave of the Kingdom of God and His Holy Spirit. He is visiting His people to shake everything that can be shaken, to tear down every idol and to remove everything to which we have looked for comfort, satisfaction and promotion outside of Him.

Oh yes, revolution is coming. Are you ready?

Be careful what you answer.

Violence

by Bonnie Beushausen

Inspired by the sermon "War and Peace: Ears to Hear in a Violent World," preached by Dr. Kim Maas on February 22, 2015, in Springfield, Missouri.

> Orange and black against a sea of blue and a sky of grey
> As 21 men of the cross gave themselves to a violent
>   death
> And hold tightly to a violent love
> Loving not their lives unto death
> As the red of their blood mingled with the waters of
>   the sea
> That follow the God of Love's design
> Washing only to the shore and no further
> Blood and water mingled together
> Onto sands that represent the number of those
> Who love with a violent love.
>
> What shall we do with a violent hate,
> With swords and guns in the name of a God

Who is Prince of Peace?
Shall we cower in fear and call to the storming skies
"Are You the One, or shall we wait for another?"
Or shall we take no offense
    And have ears to hear
Standing in violent peace
Proclaiming a violent love with a violent faith
As His violent grace and mercy are shown in our lives?

Will we joyfully proclaim His Gospel of peace
When the world around us is crumbling apart
With wars and rumors of wars
With lost jobs and failing marriages and sons we
    cannot reach?

Our battle is not one of flesh and blood
    As we sit on our recliners
Watching a line of black and orange march along a
    beach
    In perfect high definition
    . . . At least not yet.
Be it true flesh and blood with knives at our backs
Or spiritual knives as we make ultimate choices
Between comfort and warfare
    Between compromise and truth
    Between complacency and awakening
We are in the same danger of losing our lives
We are at war and must fight.

For if today while driving home
Or because our hearts give out from overindulgence
We must stand before our God of violent love
And tell Him what we did with His Son
Let it not be that we lost sight of Him
As we grew fat with our Sunday meals of feel good
    "worship"

And sermons that tickled our ears and fed not our
    souls
As we chose to fill our minds with mindless fill
From a box that takes center stage in our homes
Instead of filling our minds with things from above
    Instead of seeking intimacy with Him
    Instead of choosing to be a violent one who takes it
      by force.

The Kingdom of God suffers violence
    . . . And we can no longer play church.

We must be in violent pursuit of Him
We must be violent in showing Him
Violent peace
    Violent faith
    Violent grace
We must be the People of the Cross.

Notes

Introduction

1. Leland Ryken et al., *Dictionary of Biblical Imagery* (Downers Grove, Ill.: InterVarsity, 2000), 871–872.

Chapter 1: Are You the One?

1. See Isaiah 40:3; Matthew 3:3; Mark 1:2; Luke 3:4; John 1:23; and Luke 1:76. Elizabeth was barren. An angelic messenger announced to Zechariah that Elizabeth would conceive a child who would be great (fulfilling the prophecies of Isaiah 40:3 and Malachi 3:1; 4:6) and that he was to call his son John.

2. Abraham J. Heschel, *The Prophets* (Peabody, Mass.: Prince Press, 2004), xi–xiii.

3. James Hastings et al., *Dictionary of the Bible* (New York: Charles Scribner's Sons, 1909), 343–346.

4. R. T. Frances, "The Gospel of Matthew," *The New International Commentary on the New Testament* (Grand Rapids.: Eerdmans, 2007), 84–85.

5. Randy Clark, "The Scandal of Christianity," *Connect Quarterly Partner Magazine*, July 2019, 16.

6. Donald Juel, "Messiah," *Eerdmans Dictionary of the Bible*, ed. David Noel Freedman (Grand Rapids: Eerdmans, 2000), 890.

7. Nijay K. Gupta, "Christology," *The Lexham Bible Dictionary*, ed. John D. Barry et al. (Bellingham, Wash.: Lexham, 2016).

8. J. Jeremias, ZNW, 28 (1929), 320; also *Hat d. älteste Christenheit die Kindertaufe geübt?* (1938), 9–12.

Chapter 2: The Great Temptation

1. Σκανδαλίζω or *skandalízō* in simplest definition means to be offended at someone so as to doubt or reject them. Gustav Stählin, "Σκάνδαλον, Σκαν-δαλίζω," *Theological Dictionary of the New Testament*, ed. Gerhard Kittel, Geoffrey W. Bromiley, and Gerhard Friedrich (Grand Rapids: Eerdmans, 1964), VII: 339.

2. Colin Brown, gen. ed., *New International Dictionary of New Testament Theology*, vol. 2, (Grand Rapids: Zondervan, 1986), 707–710.

3. C. S. Lewis, "God in the Dock," *God in the Dock: Essays on Theology and Ethics*, ed. Walter Hooper (Grand Rapids: Eerdmans, 1970), loc. 3098, Kindle.

Chapter 3: Ears to Hear

1. Adam Augustyn and the editors of Encyclopaedia Britannica, "Allusion," Britannica, https://www.britannica.com/art/allusion.

2. N. T. Wright, *Matthew for Everyone, Part 1: Chapters 1–15* (London: Society for Promoting Christian Knowledge, 2004), 133–134.

3. A message from the Lord that comes through a vision or a dream can come in the form of a pun, a play on words or symbolism.

Chapter 4: The Least in the Kingdom

1. Cadillac, "2015 Cadillac ATS TV Commercial, 'Season Shifts,'" iSpot. tv, 2015, https://www.ispot.tv/ad/AVnr/2015-cadillac-ats-season-shifts.

2. F. F. Bruce, "The Epistle to the Hebrews," *The New International Commentary of the New Testament* (Grand Rapids: Eerdmans, 1990), 9.

3. This section is a modification of chapter 2 of Kim Maas, *Prophetic Community: God's Call for All to Minister in His Gifts* (Minneapolis: Chosen, 2019), 35–48.

Chapter 5: Conflict Is Unavoidable

1. R. T. France, *Matthew: The Tyndale New Testament Commentaries*, ed. Leon Morris (Downers Grove, Ill.: InterVarsity, 1985), 195–196.

2. J. B. Green, Scot McKnight, and I. Howard Marshall, eds., *Dictionary of Jesus and the Gospels* (Downers Grove, Ill.: InterVarsity).

3. Gregory Boyd, *Understanding Spiritual Warfare: Four Views*, ed. Paul Rhodes Eddy and James K. Beilby (Grand Rapids: Baker Academic, 2012), 133–137.

4. Boyd, *Understanding Spiritual Warfare*, 135.

5. Boyd, *Understanding Spiritual Warfare*, 139.

6. Clinton E. Arnold, *3 Crucial Questions about Spiritual Warfare*, ed. Grant R. Osborne and Richard J. Jones Jr. (Grand Rapids: Baker Academic, 1997), 20.

7. "Biazo," Bible Study Tools, https://www.biblestudytools.com/lexicons /greek/kjv/biazo.html.

8. Joni Eareckson Tada, Good Reads, https://www.goodreads.com/quotes /10253556-gradually-the-unthinkable-becomes-tolerable-then-acceptable -then-legal-then.

9. Do not give in to shame and condemnation. Jesus forgives sin immediately and completely. Repenting of sin is for the purpose of receiving the life that Jesus died to give us so that we can fulfill the purpose for which we were created.

Chapter 6: Kingdom Violence

1. Jon Ruthven, *What's Wrong with Protestant Theology? Traditions vs. Biblical Emphasis* (Tulsa: Word and Spirit, 2012), 151.

2. Elizabeth Nash and Joerg Dreweke, "The U.S. Abortion Rate Continues to Drop: Once Again, State Abortion Restrictions Are Not the Main Drive," Guttmacher Institute, September 18, 2019, https://www.guttmacher.org /gpr/2019/09/us-abortion-rate-continues-drop-once-again-state-abortion -restrictions-are-not-main#.

3. "Abortion Statistics," National Right to Life, http://www.nrlc.org/up loads/factsheets/FS01AbortionintheUS.pdf.

4. "Key Reasons for Passing the Born-Alive Abortion Survivors Protection Act," United States Conference of Catholic Bishops, April 2019, https:// www.usccb.org/about/pro-life-activities/upload/Born-Alive-Basics.pdf; and Lori Robertson, "The Facts on the Born-Alive Debate," FactCheck.org, March 4, 2019, https://www.factcheck.org/2019/03/the-facts-on-the-born-alive -debate/.

5. "Investigative Footage," The Center for Medical Progress, https://www .centerformedicalprogress.org/cmp/investigative-footage/.

6. Kirsten Weir, "Worrying Trends in U.S. Suicide Rates," American Psychological Association, March 2019, https://www.apa.org/monitor/2019 /03/trends-suicide.

7. Michael L. Brown, *Jezebel's War with America: The Plot to Destroy Our Country and What We Can Do to Turn the Tide* (Lake Mary, Fla.: Frontline Charisma, 2019), 44.

8. National Center of Sexual Exploitation, "Pornography and Public Health Research Summary," National Center of Sexual Exploitation (website), August 2, 2017, http://endsexualexploitation.org/wp-content/uploads/NCOSE_Porn ography-PublicHealth_ResearchSummary_8-2_17_FINAL-with-logo.pdf.

9. "20 Mind-Blowing Stats about the Porn Industry and Its Underage Consumers," Fight the New Drug, December 4, 2020, https://fightthenewdrug .org/10-porn-stats-that-will-blow-your-mind.

10. Brown, *Jezebel's War with America*, 50.

11. "The Disturbing Connection between Foster Care and Child Sex Trafficking," National Council of Juvenile and Family Court Judges, December 7, 2019, https://www.ncjfcj.org/events/the-disturbing-connection-between -foster-care-and-child-sex-trafficking.

12. "32 Shocking Divorce Statistics," McKinley Irvin Family Law, updated 2020, https://www.mckinleyirvin.com/family-law-blog/2012/october/32-shocking-divorce-statistics.

13. Bianca Bosker, "Why Witchcraft Is on the Rise," *Atlantic*, March 2020, https://www.theatlantic.com/magazine/archive/2020/03/witchcraft-juliet-diaz/605518/; and Barna Group, "Tracking the Growth and Decline of Religious Segments: The Rise of Atheism," Barna, January 14, 2020, https://www.barna.com/rise-of-atheism.

14. Jason Koutsoukis, "Indian Burning Brides and Ancient Practice on the Rise," *Sydney Morning Herald*, January 21, 2015, https://www.smh.com.au/world/india-burning-brides-and-ancient-practice-is-on-the-rise-20150115-12r4j1.html.

15. Girls Not Brides, "Ending Child Marriage in Africa," Girls Not Brides (website), https://www.girlsnotbrides.org/wp-content/uploads/2015/02/Child-marriage-in-Africa-A-brief-by-Girls-Not-Brides.pdf.

16. Chris Harris, "Girlfriend of Man who Allegedly Shot, Killed 5-Year-Old N.C. Boy on Bike Is Also Charged," *People*, September 25, 2020, https://people.com/crime/girlfriend-man-who-allegedly-shot-killed-5-year-old-neighbor-charged.

17. Boyd, *Understanding Spiritual Warfare*, 139.

Chapter 7: War and Peace

1. Paul Martini, personal conversation, 2017. Read more about peace in Paul Martini, *Accessing and Releasing God's Peace: From Chaos and Confusion to Freedom and Power* (Minneapolis: Chosen, 2019).

2. Ewelina U. Ochab, "Persecuted Christians Are Not Given Much Hope in 2020," *Forbes*, February 18, 2020, https://www.forbes.com/sites/ewelinaochab/2020/02/18/persecuted-christians-are-not-given-much-hope-in-2020/#13ec444a6889.

3. N. T. Wright, *John for Everyone, Part 2: Chapters 11–21* (London: Society for Promoting Christian Knowledge, 2004), 89.

4. Walter Grundmann, "Θαρρέω (θαρσέω)," *Theological Dictionary of the New Testament*, ed. Gerhard Kittel, Geoffrey W. Bromiley, and Gerhard Friedrich (Grand Rapids: Eerdmans, 1964), 26.

5. Kristy Huseby, "If You Want Peace, Prepare for War," The Life, https://thelife.com/if-you-want-peace-prepare-for-war.

Chapter 8: Perfect Peace

1. G. Walters and B. A. Milne, "Salvation," *New Bible Dictionary*, ed. D. R. W. Wood et al. (Downers Grove, Ill.: InterVarsity Press, 1996), 1049–1050.

2. Peter G. Bolt, *The Cross from a Distance: Atonement in Mark's Gospel*, ed. D. A. Carson, vol. 18, New Studies in Biblical Theology (Downers Grove, Ill.: InterVarsity Press, 2004), 142–143.

3. Mark J. Keown, *Discovering the New Testament: An Introduction to Its Background, Theology, and Themes: The Gospels & Acts*, vol. I (Bellingham, Wash.: Lexham, 2018), 140–141.

4. Colin Brown, ed., *New International Dictionary of New Testament Theology*, vol. 2 (Grand Rapids: Zondervan, 1986), 777.

Chapter 9: Death Has Lost Its Sting

1. Ryken, *Dictionary of Biblical Imagery*, 871–872.

2. D. W. Amundson, *New Dictionary of Theology*, ed. Sinclair B Ferguson, David F. Wright and J. I. Packer (Downers Grove, Ill.: InterVarsity, 1988), 669.

3. George Eldon Ladd, *The Gospel of the Kingdom: Scriptural Studies in the Kingdom of God* (Grand Rapids: Eerdmans, 1959), 89.

4. Alan Hawkins, unpublished unnamed sermon manuscript, Albuquerque, New Mexico, May 18, 2020.

Chapter 10: We Are the Violent

1. G. K. Chesterton, *Saint Thomas Aquinas* (San Rafael, Calif.: Angelico, 2011), 6.

2. This section on grace has been adapted from my earlier book, *Prophetic Community*. A more detailed explanation of good works can be found in endnote 2. Maas, *Prophetic Community*, 112–113, 126, 189.

Conclusion

1. Aimee Semple McPherson, "This is My Task," Foursquare.org, https://resources.foursquare.org/audio/aimee-semple-mcphersons-classic-sermon-this-is-my-task.

Kim Maas is a sought-after international speaker, author and Christian minister. After a radical encounter with the Holy Spirit on March 22, 1994, Kim left her twenty-two-year nursing career to serve God full-time. Her passion is to inspire, encourage and equip God's people to move forward in His call on their lives. This passion comes through in her preaching, leadership, writing and everyday life. Kim has trained and equipped churches, ministries and individuals to operate in the gift of prophecy in the United States and in several other nations. She served as a pastor in the local church for many years before becoming a full-time itinerate minister. She is the president and CEO of Kim Maas Ministries, the founder and director of Women of Our Time, the host of the *Move Forward with Dr. Kim Maas* podcast, and author of *Prophetic Community* published by Chosen Books. She can be heard each month live on social media with the *Voice of the Shepherds* and is a monthly featured guest with Igniting a Nation Broadcasting Network's "Prophetic Insights with Dr. Kim Maas." Kim is ordained with the International Church of the Foursquare Gospel and the Apostolic Network of Global Awakening. She earned a master of divinity at King's University and a doctorate in ministry at United Theological Seminary. Kim and her husband, Mike, live in Athol, Idaho. They have three children and a growing number of grandchildren.

You can connect with Kim at www.kimmaas.com, on Instagram @kimmaasministries, on Twitter @pkmaas, on Facebook @MoveforwardNowKimMaas and by email at hello@kimmaas .com.

More from Kim M. Maas

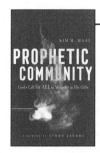

All God's people have been given the ability not only to hear His voice, but also to speak His words. Kim Maas unpacks the history of the prophetic movement, unravels misconceptions about prophecy, and explains from Scripture how prophetic community fits into God's Kingdom plan. It's time for the whole Church to step into her calling as a prophetic community!

Prophetic Community